PRAYER, THE SEARCH
FOR AUTHENTICITY

Prayer, the Search for Authenticity

PAUL HINNEBUSCH, O.P.

SHEED AND WARD : NEW YORK

© *Sheed and Ward, Inc., 1969*
Library of Congress Catalog Card Number 77–8976
Standard Book Number 8362–0227–9
Manufactured in the United States of America

INTRODUCTION

The purpose of this book is to point out some pathways toward an authentic contemporary spirituality. We do not propose to treat exhaustively of every element in the spiritual life, but rather to open up perspectives which will help contemporary man to a deeper understanding of himself as a "man of the Spirit" (cf. 1 Cor. 2:15).

The particular aspects of the spiritual life which we have chosen to treat are ones which are widely called into question in this era of growing secularization and increasing mistrust of prayer and cult. We hope that our insights will make a contribution to the solution of the current questioning and conflicts in these areas.

Our theme is the intimate relationship between prayer and life: how true prayer becomes incarnate in life and life becomes a living prayer, but only through prayer and conscience working together as one. Prayer and conscience, working as a team, are the fashioners of authentic spirituality.

Prayer and conscience become so intimately one in their cooperation that the functioning of a rightly-formed conscience tends to become ever more truly a prayer, while true prayer works for ever greater purity and clarity and sureness of conscience.

Prayer and life, then, merge into one living reality through the mediation of a rightly-formed conscience. And prayer-incarnate-in-life is spirituality.

Perhaps the whole book is best summed up in the opening sentence of Chapter 4: "We live the way we pray and we pray the way we live." The entire book grew out of that chapter, which was originally a conference given to a group of young religious in response to the problems which were agitating them. That these were indeed the widely debated problems of spirituality in our times became very clear to the author a few months later when he taught a course in spirituality in the Graduate School of Theology at the University of Notre Dame (Summer, 1968). With the desire of making the course existential, on the opening day he asked the students to write down what they considered the number one problem in their personal spirituality.

These problems, as presented by the students, have influenced in no small way the topics we have chosen to treat and have also helped in the formulation of the concept of spirituality which we present in this book. Throughout this volume, except where otherwise indicated, we have used *The Holy Bible, Revised Standard Version*. The other versions, when used, are indicated with a letter immediately after the reference, as follows:

a—*Anchor Bible*

c—Confraternity Version

d—Douay-Rheims

j—*The Jerusalem Bible*

k—*The New Testament,* translated by James Aloysius Kleist, S.J., and Joseph L. Lilly, C.M.

nc—*The New English Missal*

s—*The New Testament,* translated by Francis Aloysius Spencer, O.P.

When the documents of Vatican II are quoted, the citation is followed immediately by the initials of the first two Latin words of the document, and the number of the paragraph quoted; e.g. (*DH* 4).

Symbols of the documents quoted:

DH—Declaration on Religious Freedom (*Dignitatis Humanae*)

GS—Pastoral Constitution on the Church in the Modern World (*Gaudium et Spes*)

LG—Dogmatic Constitution on the Church (*Lumen Gentium*)

NA—Declaration on the Relationship of the Church to Non-Christian Religions (*Nostra Aetate*)

PO—Decree on the Life and Ministry of Priests (*Presbyterorum Ordinis*)

We wish to express our heartfelt gratitude to Sister Mary Henry Soniat, O.P., of St. Mary's Dominican High School, New Orleans, Louisiana, for typing the manuscript and for many valuable suggestions both as to content and expression.

ACKNOWLEDGEMENTS

The Scripture quotations in this publication (unless otherwise noted) are from the Revised Standard Version of the Bible, copyrighted 1946 and 1952 by the Division of Christian Education of the National Council of the Churches of Christ in the U.S.A., and used by permission.

Excerpts from *Proverbs and Ecclesiastes (Anchor Bible)*, translated and edited by R. B. Y. Scott. Copyright © 1965 by Doubleday & Company, Inc.

Excerpts from the *Holy Bible*, and the revised version of the *New English Missal*, copyright 1962 by the Confraternity of Christian Doctrine.

Excerpts from *The Jerusalem Bible*, copyright 1966 by Doubleday & Company, Inc.

Excerpts from *The New Testament*, translated by Francis

Aloysius Spencer, O.P., copyright 1937 by The Macmillan Company.

Excerpts from *The Summa Theologica of St. Thomas Aquinas.* First Complete American Edition, literally translated by Fathers of the English Dominican Province (New York: Benziger, 1947).

Chapter Four, "Existential Prayer," originally appeared in *Cross and Crown,* March, 1968, under the title "Prayer and Life." It is reprinted here with permission of the Editor.

CONTENTS

Introduction   *v*

Part One

PRAYER AND CONSCIENCE: SEARCH FOR
FULFILLMENT IN COMMUNION WITH GOD   **3**

1 Prayer: Life's Quest   **5**
2 Prayer: Faith Searching for Meaning   **12**
3 Prayer: A Gift from God   **20**
4 Existential Prayer   **27**
5 The Spirituality of Self-Esteem   **38**

Part Two

THE GENESIS AND DEFINITION OF
SPIRITUALITY   **55**

6 Prayer and Conscience: Fashioners of
  Spirituality   **57**

7 The need for a Criterion of Spirituality   64
8 Word and Spirit: Criteria of Spirituality   73
   I.   *Righteousness: Authentic Spirituality*   73
   II. *Conscience and the Incarnate Word*   78
   III. *The Word of God: Judgment and Gospel*   83
   IV. *The Holy Spirit: Supreme Norm of*
        Spirituality   88
9 Spirituality: Life in the Spirit   90
10 Is Spirituality One or Many?   100

Part Three
AUTHENTIC MAN: THE INVARIABLES
OF CHRISTIAN SPIRITUALITY   109
11 Authentic Man: Son of the Father   111
12 Authentic Man: Servant of His Brothers   118
13 Authentic Man: In Communion with the
   Father   124
14 The Invariables of Christian Spirituality   130

Part Four
THE MERGING OF CONSCIENCE AND
PRAYER   151
15 Conscience: Love's Quest   153
16 Conscience: Where We Meet God   166
17 The Merging of Conscience and Faith   177
18 The Spirit of Wisdom in Our "Heart
   of Hearts"   185

Part Five
"BE RENEWED IN THE SPIRIT OF
YOUR MIND"   193
19 Love's Insight and Decision   195
20 Love's Reverence   203
21 Maturity—in the Spirit   212
22 Saying Yes to God   221

Contents

23 "Redeeming the Time"   229
24 The Compatibility of Authentic Prayer
   and Human Sinfulness   237
25 From Implicit to Explicit Prayer   245
26 Be Spirited in the Spirit   256
27 "They Will Soar as with Eagles' Wings"   263

PRAYER, THE SEARCH
FOR AUTHENTICITY

Part One

PRAYER AND CONSCIENCE: SEARCH FOR FULFILLMENT IN COMMUNION WITH GOD

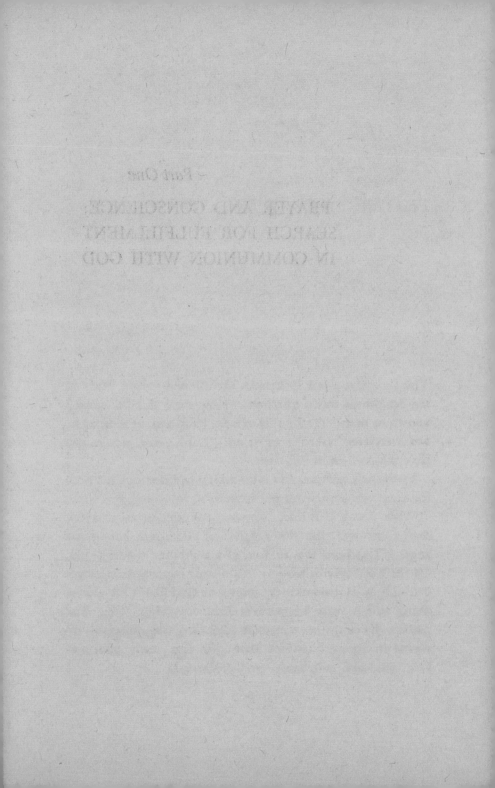

1

PRAYER: LIFE'S QUEST

The very first word spoken by the Blessed Virgin Mary in the Scriptures was a question: "How shall this be, since I know not man?" (Luke 1:34, d). St. Paul, too, as soon as he was converted, asked a question: "Lord, what would you have me do?" (Acts 22:10, d).

Everyone's spiritual life is an asking of questions, a search for meaning, a quest for the fullness of existence.

When Isaiah II is told, "Cry out," at once he asks, "What shall I cry out?" (Isa. 40:6, c). When Gideon is told by the angel, "The Lord is with you, O Champion," Gideon asks, "If the Lord is with us, why has all this happened?" (Judges 6:12–13, c). Habakkuk, too, questions God about his way of doing things, why he permits injustice (Hab. 1–2). The psalms, dialogues between man and God, are especially insistent in asking questions about life and death, man and God, good and evil, justice and injustice.

5

By nature man is a questioner. Indeed, his nature itself is a question, a quest. Man's whole being is a search for something, and that is why he asks questions.

When Moses is called by God, he asks several questions: about himself and about God. *"Who am I* that I should go to Pharao and lead the Israelites out of Egypt?" He does not dare to say to God directly, *"Who are you?"* He asks it indirectly: "When I go to the Israelites and say to them, 'The God of your fathers has sent me to you,' if they ask me, 'What is his name?' what am I to tell them?" (Exod. 3:11, 13, c).

Whether he knows it or not, in seeking understanding of himself—"Who am I?"—man is seeking understanding of God—"Who are you?"

Prayer as Search for Meaning

The most basic form of prayer is petition, an asking for something. And in this sense, man's very being is a kind of prayer. His whole being is an appeal, a crying out for what it needs. Because of himself man is a search for something not clearly known, he asks questions before he prays for definite things.

Prayer is thus first of all a search for meaning. The basic questions which man asks about his life arise as soon as he becomes aware that his whole being is a thirst. The very questioning is somehow already a prayer, for whether a man realizes it or not, his questioning is really a search for God, for only in God does man find his real answer, the meaning of his existence. His very being is directedness to God, and he is empty till he is filled with him. "Thou hast made us for thyself, O God, and our hearts are restless till they rest in thee." To the extent that he is empty, man's being is a seeking, an asking, an implicit prayer.

Prayer and Conscience

Explicit prayer begins when man becomes aware that he is a quest and accepts that fact, and in the dawning consciousness that somehow he has a responsibility to find the right answers, begins to ask questions in sincerity. Thus the dawning of prayer coincides with the dawning of conscience. Sensing his responsibility to become what he ought to be—a responsibility to someone other than himself—he seeks the right answers concerning what he is and should be.

Conscience is not primarily a passing of judgment upon past actions concerning their goodness or badness; it is first of all reason's positive search for the right actions to be performed, under the natural impulse of man's nature to become what he ought to be. The basic desire of man's will is toward this fulfillment. His will obliges his reason to search for the truth of his life—the true self he ought to be—and therefore to seek the true action, the right action, the good action which will bring him to this fulfillment. Conscience is thus an obligating power built into man's very being. It is an obligation to be what he ought to be. Conscience is but the functioning, through reason and will, of his natural thrust toward authentic fulfillment.

Conscience: a Quest

Conscience, like prayer, is thus a quest, a search for the truth of life, a seeking to measure, in one's actions, true to what one ought to be.

This conscientious search for the true action is a kind of prayer, an expression of desire; for "prayer is the interpreter of desire."[1]

Man's honest acceptance of his neediness, then, and the sincere and responsible search for his fulfillment, is a basic sort of prayer. It is an asking—even if the man is not yet very clear in his mind about the One of whom he is asking questions, about the One to whom he is responsible.

His search, as some sort of consciousness of his need of another, is more fully a prayer when it becomes a willing acceptance of this dependence upon that Other. This springs into explicitly asking him for help. The acceptance of dependence opens the way for fuller communion.

The sincerity of the quest for the answers to life is itself a basic openness to the truth of life, a willingness to accept whatever needs to be done or avoided in order to become one's true self, the self one ought to be. It is likewise a humble openness of heart, a readiness to receive whatever one needs in this process; an openness to receiving the fulfillment which is a gift from God—the gift which is God himself.

Thus prayer springs from the very texture of one's existence.

Poverty of Spirit: Humble Quest

This sincere openness, we said, is already a prayer. It is itself an appeal to God, an invitation to him who "gives grace to the humble" but "resists the proud" (Jas. 4:6, c).

This quest in sincerity, this poverty of spirit, this acknowledged neediness before God joined with hope in him, should become the basic attitude of one's personality; it should be

[1] St. Thomas Aquinas, *Summa Theologica*, IIa–IIae, Q. 83, a. 1, ad 1.

one's conscious and permanent fundamental relationship
with God; it should be the foundation of one's whole spirituality.

For prayer is the recognizing and accepting of one's various
relationships with God. And spirituality is the conscious and
willing living of these relationships.

Fidelity to Conscience: Continuing Prayer

As life's quest and questioning continues in sincerity of
heart, prayer becomes ever richer. For if the sincere acceptance of one's neediness before God is itself a prayer, then
the wholehearted acceptance of every answer to one's quest
is a perfecting of prayer. Prayer deepens as one lives true to
this basic sincerity by conscientiously, willingly accepting
each new answer; for when the prayer which is an asking of
questions receives an answer, the acceptance of the answer
by conscience brings one closer to the success of life's quest.
If prayer in its beginnings is the cry of neediness, prayer in
its completion is the possession and enjoyment of what one
needed: God. If prayer at first is a sincere asking, in the end
it is full possession and joyous communion with him for
whom we were asking, him for whom our whole being was
ever a quest, a prayer.

But there are many intermediate stages of prayer before
this fulfillment of our quest. For before we possess and enjoy
God, the final Answer, in our questioning we are given many
necessarily intermediate answers. For, we said, the working
of right conscience in seeking to know what ought to be done
is itself a prayer, an openness of heart. But if our life as a
quest is to remain a prayer, then each answer we receive,
each new discovery of truth to be done, must be willingly

accepted and carried out. Only thus will our heart remain
open, only thus will our heart open wider to receive the next
answer, only thus will our life remain a living prayer, an
openness to God, an openness to receive him as our ultimate
fulfillment.

Therefore a life according to a sincere conscience is, in a
sense, a continuing prayer. That is why we said that the
wholehearted acceptance of every answer to one's quest, the
acceptance of every discovery of conscience, is a perfecting of
prayer.

Any refusal of the truth, any rejection of the discoveries of
conscience about what is to be done, is a closing of the heart,
a rejection of the light, a loss of the way to God, the Answer
to the question of life. A life contrary to conscience is the
destruction of prayer, a blocking of the way to divine communion. When that is the situation, only the prayer of repentance, the humble cry for forgiveness, can obtain a re-
opening of the way.

Fidelity to conscience becomes ever more explicitly prayer;
for as it rightly develops, conscience becomes ever more fully
a consciousness of God, and action according to conscience
is an acceptance of God and a communion with him; it is an
openness to receive his gift of ever deeper communion.

Love's Questioning

Mary's asking of questions at the Annunciation was a seeking
of answers on a far more advanced level than the basic quest
we have been considering thus far; we have been looking
chiefly at the fundamental questioning concerning the meaning of life itself.

Mary's question, however, sprang from a wholehearted devotion to the God whom she already knew and loved greatly. Her love's readiness was asking God how his will for her was to be accomplished, how she might be at his service. Her questioning was not on the basic level of concern for her own needs, it was not a quest for her personal fulfillment; it was entirely out of love for God and concern for his will, his plan of salvation. Her personal fulfillment, of course, would be found in the accomplishment of his will for her.

In her questioning, which was an eagerness to be of service to the Lord, Mary expressed one of the basic relationships of man to God, that of servant to the Lord. When her question received its answer, and she saw clearly what was expected of her, she confirmed this relationship, she deepened it, saying, "Behold, I am the handmaid of the Lord; let it be to me according to your word" (Lk. 1:38).

2

PRAYER: FAITH SEARCHING
FOR MEANING

Prayer, we said before, begins with man's utter poverty and
neediness. Prayer, we say now, begins with God's love. Any
seeming contradictions in the two positions will be reconciled
in the following chapter.

The Christian life of each one of us begins in the same
way that Christ's own life began. This way is revealed to us
in the story of the Annunciation.

It all began with divine love. "God so loved the world
that he gave his only Son" (Jn. 3:16). This love showed itself
gracious to men. And first of all to Mary, and through her
to us. "Rejoice, so highly favored! The Lord is with you. . . .
Do not be afraid, Mary, for you have found favor with God"
(Lk. 1:28, j; 1:31). God's love has taken the initiative in
showing you his favor; it is not you who have first loved
God, it is God who has first loved you (cf. 1 Jn. 4:10).

This gratuitous divine love brings to Mary a word of vocation, a word of mission. "Behold, you will conceive in your womb and bear a son, and you shall call his name Jesus" (Lk. 1:31).

And Mary asks a question. "How shall this be?" Her question implies her love's readiness to carry out her mission. It is not a question arising from doubt, like Zachary's question, "How shall I know this?" Mary's question springs from faith. It is faith seeking understanding. Her faith has accepted the message and, in love's readiness to cooperate in its fulfillment, asks how it will be implemented.

Faith Seeking Understanding

For a word of divine vocation calling a person to fulfillment, a word of mission and the task it brings, is always a divine mystery transcending human understanding, too big for articulation in human thoughts and words. And yet, in the very nature of the case, he who receives from divine love such a word of grace and mission searches to understand it.

For by his very nature as rational, man searches for the meaning of his life. He is not an animal living by blind instinct but one who must act as a person, seeking and choosing his way by reason. Nor can he live his divine faith and vocation unless he finds its meaning in human terms. Divine revelation to man, giving him the answers he seeks in his neediness, has to be translated into the concepts of human experience before it can be lived. Revelation cannot achieve its purpose until it is grasped to some extent in human thought patterns, so that there can be a human response to it.

Whenever any man experiences a divine grace, spontaneously he tries to understand it, he seeks to conceptualize it, he tries to interpret it in terms of his previous human experiences. His experiences of grace are not fully human until he has made them his own in a human, personal way, articulating them for himself as best he can in human images and ideas. This is because every grace calls for a response, every grace brings a responsibility, and one cannot respond till he has some degree of understanding of what sort of response and action is expected. "How can this be?" Mary asks Gabriel. "Lord, what will you have me do?" Paul asks Jesus when he has received the blinding grace of conversion. Faith always seeks understanding.

Faith, searching for the fuller meaning of one's divine vocation, undertakes a new quest aroused by the initiative of God's love, a supernatural quest built into and perfecting the questioning which is man's very being. By God's call, the natural thirst for fulfillment is perfected in a new, divine thirst. And through the Holy Spirit's gift of understanding, one's faith ever more deeply penetrates the meaning of life, and especially of one's personal life. One comes to understand that life which begins as a quest ends, if the quest has been successful, in full communion with God present among us.

This meaning of life is indicated to us in the Annunciation.

The Mystery of Faith: God-with-us

When Mary's faith asks questions, "How shall this be?" the understanding granted to her is a penetration of the mystery of the Incarnation, the Word-made-man": "God-with-us!"

> The Holy Spirit will come upon you,
>   and the power of the Most High will overshadow you;
> therefore the child to be born
>   will be called holy,
>   the Son of God (Lk. 1:35).

Mary did not penetrate the full meaning of this mystery then and there. Her faith reached full understanding only after much contemplative pondering in her heart. Our faith too, searching for the meaning of life, finds the answer together with Mary. Divine love, on his own gracious initiative, has chosen to dwell with us and in us, just as he dwelt in Mary, his living temple, and with her in the daily human existence at Nazareth. Man's life, a quest and a questioning, finds the answer in God's presence among us. God's People, shown forth in Mary, type of the Church, is the temple of the living God (Apoc. 21:3). As the cloud overshadowed the tabernacle in the desert of Sinai and the glory of God—the divine Presence—filled it (Exod. 40:34), so by the overshadowing of the Holy Spirit, Mary (and after her and with her, the Church) has been filled with the indwelling God.

Thus the quest which began as man's search to understand *himself* becomes faith seeking to understand and possess *God*. For, like Moses, every man asks questions about himself and about God, since the quest to understand self is really a search to understand God. Only in the understanding of God does man at last understand himself; for his very nature is thirst for God, desire for the vision of God. He understands himself in the understanding of God as love—love communicating himself, God as given to man, God as revealed in the very gift of himself: God-with-us.

The Incarnational Hidden Life

Our spiritual life begins, then, with God's love favoring us with an inner divine word of vocation, and on earth this life is fulfilled with God's presence among us in the ordinary everyday existence of man.

Such is the mystery of the annunciation and incarnation at Nazareth. Not in the sacred place, the Temple at Jerusalem where he appeared to Zachary, did Gabriel speak to Mary. He came to her in the midst of her everyday home life at Nazareth, and into that ordinary human existence she received the Son of God.

Our faith too, like Mary's, pondering and questioning, searching for meaning, comes to understand the truth of Nazareth, "the hidden life," the life hidden with Christ in God (Col. 3:3).

The Christian life is hidden not in the sense that the Christian withdraws from the eyes of men. On the contrary, Christ says, "Let your light so shine before men that they may see your good works and give glory to your Father who is in heaven" (Mt. 5:16). Nor is the Christian life hidden in the sense that the Christian separates himself from ordinary human life and goes into hiding in a desert. It *is* hidden in the sense that it lives a reality which is unseen except by faith—the mystery of God in our midst in our ordinary human existence, the mystery of communion with God, the mystery that we are sons of God in Christ.

"Everyone should remain in the state in which he was called," says St. Paul (1 Cor. 7:20), meaning that they should not consider life in the world of men as unholy, unsacred, in the way that the Jews had formerly considered the life of pagans unconsecrated. Wherever they are—in the ordinary affairs of daily life, in any life-situation whatever—Christians, through lively, faith enlightened by the gifts of knowledge and understanding, should penetrate to the hidden reality of their life, the reality of Christ dwelling in their hearts by faith.

This Christian reality of a life "hidden with Christ in God" (Col. 3:3) will be fully revealed only at the parousia. "When Christ who is our life appears, then you also will appear with him in glory" (Col. 3:4). Till then it will be lived in the darkness of faith, for what is lived by faith is not seen. And yet not in total darkness. For faith, searching for life's full meaning, finds it through the Holy Spirit's gifts of understanding and wisdom—understanding, which is a perfecting of faith; wisdom, which is a savoring of the divine presence. Prayer which started as a quest and a questioning is thus perfected in the prayer of full communion with the God who is with us. Thus faith experiences the hidden life, it tastes the reality of the divine presence with us. This is to live the hidden life—in the ordinary, everyday human existence, to experience the life with God, as Mary experienced the life with God in the human situation at Nazareth.

The Hidden Life and Dynamic Hope

Though this life will remain hidden till the parousia, nevertheless the hidden reality is grasped securely with certitude and conviction to the extent that one has tasted it, experienced it through the gifts of understanding and wisdom, whose fruits are certitude and joy.[2]

To say that this life is hidden in the darkness of faith is

[2] Cf. Rom. 15:13; Eph. 1:15–19; Col. 1:9–14.

not to say that it is inactive. We shall be considering in various ways the dynamic aspects of God's life within us, the "practice of the truth in love" (Eph. 4:15, c), the thrust of faith as actively at work in hope, the involvement in the world of men to which faith and love impel us.

The Hidden Life Incarnate in Everyday Existence

Life, we said, should be prayer incarnate. The divine reality which we grasp in faith—the reality of God living in us—is incarnate in the ordinary, down-to-earth daily human existence. The communion with God is embodied and expressed in a fully human way, in a human life which is lived divinely, lived with God who dwells in our hearts by faith, and who impels us to practise the truth in love in the task of Christian hope, the building up of the Body of Christ in love (Eph. 4:15–16).

The hidden life can be lived in the midst of the most active apostolate. If it really is an apostolate, a participation in Christ's own life and mission, then it is an expression or function of the Christ-life within us. The apostle can be contemplatively aware of Christ who is dwelling and working in him and through him, and thus be in contemplation in the midst of his Christian action. (By Christian action we do not mean mere activity, but action inspired by faith and love and flowing from Christ, who dwells in us.)

This action is not the cause of one's contemplation in the midst of action. For infused contemplation is ever the direct gift of the Holy Spirit. Genuine Christian action, however, helps to open one to the Spirit to receive this gift; because the self-sacrificing love required in an exacting apostolate purifies one of the obstacles to the gifts of the Spirit and surrenders one more fully to the Spirit for his light and love.

The apostle's contemplation makes his apostolate all the more fruitful, for in contemplation he is more effectively and personally united to Christ, more fully in the hands of the Spirit.

To live with Christ in God is not to be separated from our fellowmen, it is to live, like Christ, among men; and in Christ, with Christ, to seek the Father together.

3

PRAYER: A GIFT FROM GOD

In saying, in this present chapter, that prayer begins with God, that it is a gift from him, we may seem to be contradicting the theme of an earlier chapter, "Prayer, Life's Quest." There we said that the first prayer is man's poverty, his neediness, his thirst, which cries out for something. His quest to discover just what he is and therefore what he needs is a kind of prayer. He begins to ask for explicit gifts only after this quest has made some discoveries.

Prayer, then, would seem to begin with man.

But then we showed that prayer begins with God's love and favor toward men, with his word of personal vocation to one whom he has chosen. God always takes the initiative, and prayer is a response to his word of self-revelation.

Inasmuch as it is a response to God's graciousness and

grace, prayer is always at least a beginning of the communion with God which is prayer in its fullness; and communion with God can be only by his grace. The first invitations of God's gracious love, when responded to by man in fidelity and perseverance, lead ultimately to the highest prayer: God's full communication of himself to the man who is at last fully receptive through long-term faithfulness to God's repeated overtures.

Obviously, we have been using the term *prayer* in a variety of senses. When we say that our very being is a prayer, a thirst for God, we are speaking metaphorically. But we are revealing the profoundest reason for explicit prayer; man's ontic need for God. His very being is hunger for God, he is a natural desire for the beatific vision. But this ontic desire, this desire built into his very being, remains ineffective and even unconscious and incapable of fulfillment, until God takes the initiative and by a gift of grace turns the ineffective desire of nature into a fruitful supernatural desire for true communion with God.

This supernatural desire, reaching out to God in a hope which is not disappointed, is a basic element in all supernatural prayer, the prayer which alone fully deserves the name prayer, the prayer which is a gift from God and which in its fullness is full communion with God.

Only by a supernatural call of grace, only in response to some sort of interior divine word, can man effectively desire and achieve this communion with God. Without that initiative of divine grace and man's response to it, the natural desire for God which is his very being will remain an ineffective desire. "No one can come to me unless the Father who sent me draws him" (Jn. 6:44).

Thirst for Living Waters

Prayer is a thirst. Thirst for what? Our whole being is a thirst, we said, but we do not really know what we thirst for till the Holy Spirit gives us thirst for the Father in heaven.

The woman of Samaria came thirsting to Jacob's well (Jn. 4:7–15). But like Israel in the days of Jeremiah, she had been coming to broken, empty cisterns, to lovers who were unable to give her what her whole being longed for. "They went after empty idols and became empty themselves." "They have forsaken me, the source of living waters, they have dug for themselves cisterns, broken cisterns that hold no water" (Jer. 2:5, 13, c).

Jesus, taking the initiative, patiently teaches the woman to thirst for the divine waters; "If you knew the gift of God, and who it is that is saying to you, 'Give me a drink,' you would have asked him, and he would have given you living water" (Jn. 4:10). "Now this he said about the Spirit which those who believed in him were to receive" (Jn. 7:39). The very thirst for the living waters is a gift of God.

Thirst for the Father

The Holy Spirit causes thirst for the Father. The first effect of the presence of the Spirit in our hearts, the first cry he inspires in us, is "Abba!" a cry of longing and of hope which is not disappointed (Rom. 5:5; 8:15). Once we have sipped the living waters, we thirst ever more avidly to satisfy our thirst at their Source. On his way to his martyrdom in Rome, St. Ignatius of Antioch wrote, "The living water speaks within me, saying, 'Hasten to the Father!' "[3]

[3] "Letter to the Romans," *The Fathers of the Church: The Apostolic Fathers* (New York: Cima, 1947), p. 11.

Christ's own prayer on earth was a thirst for the Father. "Father, glorify thou me in thy own presence, with the glory which I had with thee before the world was made. . . . Father, I am coming to thee!" (Jn. 17:5, 11). That he eagerly desired to be with the Father is evident in his reproach to his apostles for their sadness at his departure: "If you loved me, you would have rejoiced, because I go to the Father; for the Father is greater than I" (Jn. 14:28).

To be with the Father is somehow even more important to Jesus than being with his friends on earth, his fellowmen. And, of course, he will be more useful to his friends when he is with the Father, for when he has gone to the Father, he will be able to send the Holy Spirit of adoption, who will make them, too, thirst for the Father. His whole mission in the world was to bring his fellowmen to the Father, to make them thirst for the Father, to give them the Holy Spirit inspiring the cry, "Abba!" the desire for the divine embrace.

The Search for Identity

Only in the gift of the Holy Spirit, then, does man find the answer to his search for meaning, his questions about himself, his questions about God. Only when the love of God is poured forth into his heart by the Holy Spirit who is given to him (Rom. 5:5) does he discover his identity: he is a son of God, recognizing God as Father. He knows who he is, he knows who God is.

If he has been seeking God, God has been seeking him still more. God's love created his nature as a thirst for God, but only when God's love has turned to him and has poured itself into his heart in the gift of the Holy Spirit does man

as a person effectively and ardently thirst for God in a hope
which is not disappointed (Rom. 5:5).

Prayer, then, is a gift. For only in the gift of the Holy
Spirit does the natural desire of our being become a conscious, effective, personal desire and hope for the embrace
of God our Father. The cry of poverty which is our very
being, the cry which is all the more pitiful when we do not
yet know what we are crying for, becomes a clear and explicit "Father" only when the Father pours the gift of his
Spirit into our hearts.

The cry inspired by the Spirit remains a thirst till the end,
it becomes an ever more avid thirst, as in the case of Ignatius
of Antioch: it is a longing for the full embrace of the Father
in beatific vision. And till the end it remains a cry from the
desert, a cry in the darkness, a continuing search for ever
clearer identity, for fuller understanding of self and of God
—till at last one is given "a white stone with a new name
written on the stone which no one knows except him who
receives it" (Rev. 2:17). Only then will one know fully who
he is.

For while we are still in the desert of this life, although
on the testimony of the Spirit we have the unshakable certitude that God is our Father, the Father is as yet unseen.
"Hope that is seen is not hope" (Rom. 8:24). We do not yet
know clearly what we thirst for. Therefore "the Spirit helps
us in our weakness, for we do not know how to pray as we
ought, but the Spirit himself intercedes for us with sighs too
deep for words" (Rom. 8:26).

Thus our prayer continues to be a cry of poverty, a search
for the unknown, for the unexpected, for the "inbreaking"
of God from above. But now it is a cry of hope that cannot
be disappointed; it is a prayer which begins with God and

is his continuing gift, for it is inspired in us by his indwelling Spirit.

Yes, man is seeking God, but God is seeking him still more!

Incarnate Hope

And this prayer of thirst and hope for God becomes incarnate in our whole life and action when everything we do—guided by right conscience according to his will—is directed to God in the Holy Spirit. For the forward thrust of our hope toward the Father is expressed in creative Christian action, the action in which together we cooperate with Christ in the building up of his Body, the kingdom of peace and justice and love (*GS* 39).

Our hope becomes incarnate, as it were, in this action. For unless hope does become incarnate in a life in the likeness of Christ, we have no hope.

For only the coheirs of Christ have hope of the inheritance; and the coheirs are they who have suffered with him, they who have become conformed to his likeness (Rom. 8:17), they who have built their hope, in union with the risen Christ, by their united Christian action in the Spirit.

If we are to transform our life into an incarnate prayer of hope—a life whose hope will not be disappointed because it is in reality a life of a son of God, coheir with Christ—it is essential that we cultivate thirst for the Spirit, thirst for his ever-flowing gifts of power and inspiration. For only to the extent that we "are led by the Spirit of God" can we be sons of God and brothers of one another in Christ (Rom. 8:14). Only in the Spirit can we engage in the action of sons which makes our whole life a living hope. The action which transforms, the action which is hope, is the action in the Spirit, gift of the risen Christ. The transformation of our life into an incarnate hope is the Spirit's work and ours, as we and he work together as one principle of Christian action.

And this is fraternal, cooperative action, in which the whole of human society, not just the individual Christian, is purified, illumined and transfigured in the likeness of Christ (*GS* 39), with unshaken hope for the full inheritance of glory with the Son.

We must, therefore, never lose the thirst for the Spirit, we must ever seek ardently to come completely under his control. We must beware of getting involved in activity which is not inspired by the Spirit.

Thus Christian hope is not just a cry of confident prayer in the Holy Spirit. It has become incarnate hope, hope incarnate in a life in conformity with the Paschal Lamb, a whole life which is the cry "Father," the cry of hope, a life which is ever going to the Father.

Such a life is a participation in Christ's own thirst for his Father—"Father, I am coming to thee!"—and ends in the full presence of the Father in glory. "Father, glorify thou me in thy own presence!" (Jn. 17:5).

4

EXISTENTIAL PRAYER

We live the way we pray, and we pray the way we live. The quality of our prayer-life is the test of the worth of the rest of our life, and the rest of our life reveals the quality of our prayer.

This is because prayer is not finished until it is lived. For have we really lifted our heart to God if we have not offered him our whole being? And have we really given our whole being if we do not complete the offering in our living? "This people honors me with their lips," the Lord complains, "but their heart is far from me" (Mt. 15:8). And again he says, "Not everyone who says to me, 'Lord, Lord,' shall enter the kingdom of heaven, but he who does the will of my Father who is in heaven" (Mt. 7:21). Prayer is perfected in doing —in living according to the Father's salvific will.

*True Prayer Transforms the Whole of
Existence*

Prayer is therefore never abstract, it is not something apart
from life. If it is true prayer, it springs from life, and, in
turn, is expressed and completed in life. And thus St. Paul
says, "Present your bodies [persons] as a living sacrifice, holy
and acceptable to God, which is your spiritual worship"
(Rom. 12:1). Prayer expressed in living makes our whole
existence a worship of God. Prayer, lifting mind and heart
to God in response to his word, directing and carrying the
whole of life to God as a living liturgy, is the very warp and
woof of Christian existence, the basic web into which the
rest of our existence is woven.

This is a first reason why we can say that true prayer is
existential: it penetrates and transforms the totality of our
existence. The quality of our prayer regulates the quality of
our total existence.

But a life which is thus a *lived* prayer through the influence of *prayed* prayer very readily springs again into praying
prayer, explicit prayer, prayer in the strictest sense of the
word. The quality of this renewed, explicit prayer is determined in no small way by the manner in which we have
lived our previous prayers. How we order the rest of our life
is thus of the greatest importance for prayer, for our life is
the living root from which prayer should spontaneously
spring.

Some are perhaps losing heart at this moment, thinking:
My prayer-life is so miserable that the rest of my life must
be worthless; or my life is such a confusion that my prayers
must be without value. But the seemingly miserable state
of either one's prayer or one's life could possibly be only

growing pains: one is still deeply involved in life's search for meaning. If the pains are signs of growth, if they are the signs of adjustment to life through the often painful accept-ance of the answers discovered by conscience, then they are a cause for hope, not discouragement.

The problem of how to pray, then, is the problem of how to live; and vice versa.

Prayer: Fullness of Existence

The problem of how to live is this: how to exist to the full-ness of one's capacities for existing. We can scarcely be said to exist if we are static, lifeless, not growing. The natural desire to be is a desire to be in all the fullness of existence. In any existence less than God's, this implies growth, dy-namic reaching out in hope for a level of existence tran-scending our present level.

If we accept this dynamic concept of existence, we should be able to see that we cannot fully exist unless we pray. Prayer is the stretching forth in hope to an existence or fullness of life infinitely transcending our own capacities, an existence in God, the existence for which we were created, to which we are called by the Word of God, into which only the Holy Spirit can conduct us. Prayer, whether as prayed or as lived, is a "straining forward to what lies ahead," a pressing on "toward the goal, for the prize of the upward call of God in Christ Jesus" (Phil. 3:13-14).

St. Paul ardently wanted his converts to grow in apprecia-tion of these facts about the fullness of Christian existence. He tells the Ephesians that he has been earnestly praying for them, that "having the eyes of your hearts enlightened, you may know what is the hope to which he has called you, what are the riches of his glorious inheritance in the saints, and what is the immeasurable greatness of his power in us who believe" (Eph. 1:18–19).

He tells the Romans that we stretch out to attain this glorious hope because we are inspired by the Holy Spirit dwelling within us. Because we have been obedient to the faith, "God's love has been poured into our hearts through the Holy Spirit who has been given to us . . . the Spirit himself bearing witness with our spirit that we are children of God. . . . Likewise the Spirit helps us in our weakness; for we do not know how to pray as we ought, but the Spirit himself intercedes for us with sighs too deep for words. And he who searches the hearts of men knows what is the mind of the Spirit, because the Spirit intercedes for the saints according to the will of God" (Rom. 5:5; 8:16; 8:26–27).

That is, to accomplish in us his salvific will, the Father sends his Spirit into our hearts to inspire us to desire according to that saving will, though the things we desire surpass our understanding and explicit asking.

That is why St. Paul can tell the Ephesians that by the power of the Holy Spirit, God will accomplish all things in us in a manner far surpassing our desires and expectations: "By the power at work within us [he] is able to do far more abundantly than all we ask or think" (Eph. 3:20).

The Apostle, then, wants us to be ever more conscious of the greatness of our hope, the fullness of the existence in God to which we are called; he wishes us to be conscious of and responsive to the indwelling Holy Spirit who impels us to this fullness of life, inspiring us to desire and hope for it, and to reach for it in a life daily growing up to it.

We see, then, a second reason for saying that true prayer

is always existential. We cannot fully exist unless we pray, since the fullness of human existence can be found only in God. Prayer is a reaching for that fullness, in a hope which is not disappointed (Rom. 5:5), because it is inspired by God's own Holy Spirit who has been given to us. This aspiration toward God springs from the very ground of our being, from the deepest depths of our hearts where the Holy Spirit dwells, making our life "a spring of water welling up to eternal life" (Jn. 4:15).

Prayer and Life-Situations

The problem of how to pray, then, and the problem of how to live—the two are the same problem—is the problem of becoming ever more aware of this Holy Spirit within us, and of becoming ever more responsive to him as he seeks to inspire us to embrace God's saving will.

It is a matter of learning to discern his often delicate interior inspirations, and of responding in aspiration toward the infinite hope toward which he impels us. But it is also a matter of learning to discern his presence and purpose in the various life-situations in which we find ourselves. For we can make all of life a living prayer only by seeking and embracing God's salvific will as manifest in every situation of life.

Vatican II declares that the People of God, led by the Holy Spirit and motivated by faith, "labors to decipher authentic signs of God's presence and purpose" in the events and needs of the times (*GS* 11). Not only must the Church discern the broad trends of God's purpose and grace, but each individual Christian should be able to discern what God wills to accomplish in all the situations of his personal life.

"With the light of faith" each one "can carefully detect the
signs of God's will and impulses of his grace in the various
happenings of life" (*PO* 18).

The problem of prayer and of life, then, is a matter of
saying "Yes" to all of God's invitations, whether these come
in the form of interior grace and inspiration, or whether
they are manifest in the problems and challenges inherent in
the situations of everyday living. And, of course, the two go
together. For the life-problem can be solved only in the light
given in interior grace.

We have to be able to discern God's workings in the
events of everyday life, for our life and personality develop
only in our response to the world of men and things about
us, the world in which God has placed us, the world in which
he speaks to us, the various situations in which we must learn
to discern the signs of his presence and purpose. For we
grow up to God in our everyday life in the community of our
fellowmen and in the midst of the things about us which we
use, and which influence us.

"Look carefully then how you walk, not as unwise men
but as wise, making the most of the time, because the days
are evil. Therefore do not be foolish, but understand what
the will of the Lord is" (Eph. 5:15–17).

Discerning God's Salvific Will
in Life's Situations

The problem of prayer and of life, then, is the problem of
discerning the salvific will of God at every step of our life.
God's will is always salvific; that is, his will in our regard is
ever a will of love, a will to bring us to salvation and holiness. His will is never arbitrary, it is never a sheer assertion

of authority. Anything and everything he wills for us is intended to lead us into salvation, which is life in communion with him.

We need, then, to see the saving God at work in everything. He is the ever living and loving God, here and now actively accomplishing the purposes of his love in all things, and therefore here and now present to us with his will to save, his offer of saving grace. To make all of life a living prayer, we need to discern and respond to his presence and purpose in everything which comes our way.

Every problem we encounter in life has to be seen as a problem presented to us by God himself, to be solved by us in the light given by the Holy Spirit who dwells in us. Whatever we run into in life should call from us the question: What is God asking of me in this situation? What response does he expect of me? What is his will for me, his saving will? What grace of spiritual growth is hidden in this situation, to be mine in embracing his saving will?

Each situation contains an offer of a fuller existence, a deeper life, a call to let the buds of life burst into blossom and fruit, a challenge to break out of one's narrow complacency and self-satisfaction to a greater fullness of life and holiness.

How easily we say "No" to these new invitations from God contained in every new situation of life. We are, perhaps, too satisfied with things as they are; we complacently think that we are well adjusted to life and have achieved our fullness of growth; but here comes this new crisis, calling for another difficult readjustment. And so we are inclined to resent the crisis, this interference with our complacent idea that we were good enough, mature enough, holy enough, Christian enough, or had done enough for God.

Since the horizons of Christian hope are infinite, we should never stop growing toward them, growing in holiness. And so there will always be new growing pains for any Christian who is really alive, not stagnant in complacency. We will not grow in personality and in spirituality without constant adjustments and readjustments, as we discern God anew in the new problems he presents in our life, as we choose him anew in embracing his saving, life-giving will in each new problem which comes our way.

The difficult situation or problem with which God presents us may be, for example, the presence of some person whose personality clashes with ours. "That woman!" we exclaim impatiently. "She always brings out the worst in me!"

But God's salvific will and grace wishes to save us from this worst in us. He wills that we see to it, in the presence of this jarring person, that her presence brings out, not the worst, but the best in us. And his Holy Spirit is in us to make this possible, if we will but say "Yes" to the divine challenge in the situation and respond to that person in patience and understanding, in kindness and a sincere effort to love.

God's salvific will for us, then, works in every situation. Every situation contains an offer of grace, an offer of a fuller life, a higher existence, if we will but discern this will of God and say "Yes" to it. It is not so much the situation that contains the grace. The grace is already in us in the Person of the Holy Spirit, who enables us to grow from within in response to the purpose of God's workings in all things. Whether it be overwork or a sickness, a distasteful assignment from an employer, or an exceptionally difficult apostolate, difficulties in prayer, or temptations arising from some human weakness, there is never a life-situation which does not contain an offer of divine grace to those who respond in the way God wills that they respond. Our way of meeting the situation will become a living prayer only if we have sought and found and embraced the salvific will of God revealed in the problem.

Divine Providence and Personal Responsibility

This is the deeper meaning of the scriptural doctrine of divine providence: "We know that in everything God works for good *with those* who love him, who are called according to his purpose" (Rom. 8:28). *"With those"*: if God works, that means that those who love him work also. They work together. Trust in divine providence is no mere surrender of everything into God's powerful hands while we sit back and do nothing. Trust in providence is not an abdication of responsibility; it is an embracing of God's salvific will and becoming its instrument, it is a saying "Yes" to his plan for us here and now.

Sometimes, of course, his full purpose is hidden, and no matter how hard we seek we cannot discern it clearly. But if we strive to live according to the Holy Spirit who is within us, "the Spirit helps us in our weakness . . . the Spirit himself intercedes for us with sighs too deep for words (8:26)." He inspires us to want to embrace the saving will of God which works in this situation. "And he who searches the hearts of men knows what is the mind of the Spirit, because the Spirit intercedes for the saints according to the [salvific] will of God" (Rom. 8:26–27). In some situations, then, we grope in the dark, but the Holy Spirit within us knows the way clearly.

At other times, however, what God's saving will is asking
of us is clearly evident in the situation itself, or can be found
with a certain amount of effort; for example, encountering
that person who always brings out the worst in us; God's
saving will calls for our effort in bringing out the best in
self, and bestows the grace to do so if we say "Yes" to what
he is asking. "We know that in everything God works for
good with those who love him" (Rom. 8:28).

This discerning and embracing of God's true purpose in
all of life's situations is the only possible way of encountering
God in everyone and in every event, it is the only way of
turning all of life into a genuine prayer, a true response to
God. We cannot say that our life—our works, our sufferings,
our relations with others, our eating and drinking and rec-
reation and resting—we cannot say that all of this is sanctified
and has become a living prayer, unless we have honestly
sought God's true will in every undertaking, in every frustration, and have embraced his purpose willingly. The
morning offering sanctifies our day, making it a living prayer,
only to the extent that this offering becomes effective in the
effort to discern and accomplish God's will all day long.

The morning offering really says: "Father, I will seek your
true will in everything I do today; for only that is sanctified
which is done in accordance with your will. I will strive to
live under the influence of the Holy Spirit, who will enable
me to live in the likeness of your Son who said, 'He who sent
me is with me; he has not left me alone, for I always do what
is pleasing to him' " (Jn. 8:29).

This manner of living in the presence of God by discerning his presence and purpose in every situation, this making
all our living an implicit prayer, easily blossoms forth into
explicit prayer, the full consciousness of the divine presence.

And explicit prayer, in turn, deepens the implicit prayer which is daily living. Success in explicit prayer brings greater ease in living as God would have us live, whereas many of our difficulties in explicit prayer stem from unsolved difficulties in living according to God's true will; that is, we cannot pray well because we have said "No" to God in some area or other of our daily life.

Examination of conscience, growth in self-knowledge to find these areas of resistance to God, is therefore necessary for progress in prayer.

We see, then, the meaning of our statement that the problem of how to pray is the problem of how to live; and vice versa. We pray the way we live and we live the way we pray.

5

THE SPIRITUALITY
OF SELF-ESTEEM

We have been speaking of prayer and conscience as a quest
for self-fulfillment. But is not the quest for self-fulfillment
a danger in the spiritual life? Is not self-love a constant
threat to spiritual progress and have not spiritual writers
persistently warned against it? And yet, psychologists claim
that a true love for oneself is essential to a mature and
balanced personality.

Authentic Self-Love Necessary
for True Spirituality

Were the spiritual writers wrong in attacking self-love? Not
at all. For, presupposing a healthy self-esteem as the foundation of genuine spiritual progress, they warned rather against

a false love of self, a distorted self-love which was destructive of the true love of self commanded by the Scriptures.

"My son," writes Sirach, "with humility have self-esteem and value yourself at your proper worth" (10:27, c; 10:28, j). If we do not hold ourselves in right esteem, we will dishonor ourselves in sin. Therefore, in another translation of the words just noted, Sirach says: "Glorify yourself with humility and ascribe to yourself honor according to your worth. Who will justify the man that sins against himself? And who will honor the man who dishonors his own life?" (10:28-29).

To sin is to dishonor self, it is to fail in true self-love.

Therefore, Pope Pius XII could say that self-love is necessary for morality, thus implying that lack of self-esteem is immoral. In an address to clinical psychologists in 1953, he said, "There exists in fact a defense, an esteem, a love and service of one's personal self which is not only justified but demanded by psychology and morality."[4]

The Scriptures attack the wrong kind of self-love—"He who loves his life loses it" (Jn. 12:25)—but they command the right kind: "You shall love your neighbor *as yourself*" (Mk. 12:31). Authentic self-love is thus presented as the pattern for authentic love of neighbor.

Thus, Paul VI writes in *Progressio Populorum:*

In God's plan, every man is born to seek self-fulfillment, for every human life is called to some task by God. . . . Endowed with intellect and free will, each man is responsible for his self-fulfillment even as he is for his salvation. He is helped and sometimes hindered by his teachers and those around him; yet what-

[4] Quoted by G. Donald Maloney, "Self-Esteem and the Religious," *Review for Religious,* 22 (1963), p. 435.

ever be the outside influences exerted on him, he is the chief architect of his success or failure.[5]

The primary responsibility for one's salvation and personal fulfillment, then, falls upon the person himself. And this is because he can be saved, and fulfilled as a person, only by his personal choice, only by his freedom exercised with responsibility.

Because the primary responsibility for one's salvation and fulfillment falls upon self, the love of self is even more basic than the love of neighbor. Indeed, it is so basic that it is presupposed to both love of God and of neighbor; it is so fundamental that it does not even need to be expressed explicitly in the two greatest commandments (Mk. 12:30–31). Neither God nor neighbor can be loved without a healthy self-esteem. On the other hand, one can rightly love self only by loving both God and neighbor.

Authentic self-love is truly a must in a healthy spirituality.

Psychological Self-Esteem

What then is the psychological self-esteem which is so necessary for a mature and balanced personality and which is included in the Christian self-love of which our Lord speaks?

Self-esteem can be defined as a sense of one's intrinsic self-worth.

By *intrinsic* self-worth, we mean one's value as a human person even independently of one's talents and accomplishments. For even one who is not very gifted and has few accomplishments to his credit can and must have a healthy self-esteem. We say that authentic self-love is a *sense* of one's

[5] *The Pope Speaks,* 12 (1967), p. 149.

intrinsic self-worth. For a child needs a pre-reflective consciousness of his value as a person even before he has been able to catalogue intellectually his abilities and talents, and before he has had opportunity to experience his worth through accomplishments. Moreover, every person, at any stage of his life, needs to sense his intrinsic worth even when he has been a failure in his efforts at accomplishment. He must be able to love and esteem himself more for what he *is* than for what he does or has done.

He *is* a human being, a person made in the image and likeness of God, and must ever love and value himself as such. Only this kind of self-esteem enables him to consider life worthwhile, only this sense of self-worth gives him the courage to undertake life's responsibilities, only this true self-love makes possible self-sacrifice in the love of God and neighbor. As we said, the spiritual writers who condemn false self-love are really condemning the failure to value oneself rightly. In selfishness and sin, one sells self too cheaply.

The child's sense of his intrinsic self-worth, his pre-reflective consciousness of his value as a person, presupposes that he has experienced someone's love for him. Only because he has been loved by parents and others does he have a sense of his dignity and worth as a person, and therefore the courage to love in return and to undertake the labor and self-sacrifice of loving others.

Self-esteem, then, though it can certainly become stronger through the addition of a sense of accomplishment, is first of all a response to another's love, a love which desires to make something of the loved one. The child, even before he has done anything worthy of praise, should experience someone's creative and nurturing love for him, a love which gives him a sense of his value as a person and assists in the development of this value. His whole life can thus be a love in return, trying to be worthy of this creative love. When the creative love is truly unselfish and desires that the child should become what he really ought to be, the child learns to esteem himself rightly and responds by trying to measure true to what love desires for him. In grateful love he tries to please those who love him, he tries to give joy to them. Thus his self-esteem is referred to the joy of others, he is able to love self in an unselfish way for the sake of others. He can love self with humility and gratitude, neither undervaluing himself (for he senses his personal dignity) nor overvaluing himself by attributing a false worth to himself in pride, vanity, bizarre conduct meant to attract attention, or unworthy ambition.

Esteem for Self as Child of God

If self-esteem depends at first and for a long time upon the love of parents and of others for us, till the end of life it has to depend upon a realization of God's love for us, it has to result from an experience of being loved by God as well as by men.

For the command of God that we have self-esteem is a command to appreciate *his* love for us and measure true to the dignity this love has given us in creating and redeeming us, calling us to participate in his own life as sons in his Son. Just as the child has to sense that he has a worth sheerly as a person and independently of his talents and accomplishments or lack of them, so too the child of God, to uphold him in the struggle for Christian perfection and to save him from discouragement and despair because of his sins and failures, needs a permanent conviction of his worth as created and redeemed by God.

In the story of the prodigal son (Lk. 15), the heavenly Father is saying to each one of us, "My son, with humility have self-esteem" (Sir. 10:27, c). Though we are sinners like the prodigal and may have done things which threaten our self-respect, the Father ever continues to love us and call us "my son." For though the prodigal had awakened to his sinfulness and was ready to confess it, saying, "Father, I am no longer worthy to be called thy son" (Lk. 15:19, c), the father received him as son even before he could make this confession. "While he was yet a long way off, his father saw him and was moved with compassion, and ran and fell upon his neck and kissed him" and called him son: "This my son was dead and has come to life again, he was lost and is found" (Lk. 15:20, 24, c).

Every man's whole value is summed up in that love of his heavenly Father for him which calls him "my son." For no matter how much a prodigal he is, he was created and redeemed to be a son of God, and the Father in heaven is ever ready to receive him as such.

The mere fact, then, that God loved us so much that he made and redeemed us to be his children gives us an inestimable worth which can always adequately ground our self-esteem. No matter how we may fall, we can and must ever maintain, or recover, this basic self-esteem without which repentance and conversion are impossible, the self-esteem which realizes the undying love of God for us. The sin of despair is really a proud refusal to accept God's love which loves us sinners not because we are lovable of ourselves, but because God is love. Our whole value is ever the gift of this love. "My son, with humility have self-esteem."

Even we sinners, then, can have self-esteem. "Not that we have loved God, but that he has first loved us, and sent his son a propitiation for our sins" (1 Jn. 4:10, c).

Self-Esteem Effective in Life

Any man's self-esteem, however, proves its power and depth only to the extent that it moves him to live true to his God-given worth. Self-esteem is rather weak and shallow if it remains only in the order of feeling or wishful thinking. True self-love, however, springing as it does from a conviction of God's love which values us so highly, strives to become effective in a life measuring true to what God meant us to be. We value ourselves at our true worth only when we grant his love's desire by living true to what his love would have us be—his sons!

The self-esteem called for by the Scriptures is thus no mere mental evaluation. It is lived, it is effective in our lives.

Humble self-love is thus something far removed from pride. It is humble not merely because we realize that all our worth is the gift of God's love, but because the very prizing of ourselves by living as God's sons is an honoring of God. To throw away our heritage as his sons, to disown him as our Father, is to dishonor him, to insult him. This is the height of pride. Pride is the effort to find all our worth in ourselves apart from God, according to our own will and by our own power.

But to love ourselves dearly as his sons and to desire to be perfect in love for him is not pride but humility, it is the supreme way of honoring him as our God and Father. To call him "Father!" with sincerity and understanding of all that word implies is to declare in humility that all our worth, all that we are and have, is the gift of his creative and redeeming love, his begetting love.

Christian self-esteem, then, is the opposite of pride. Enlightened by the Holy Spirit, who bears witness with our spirit that we are sons of God, we have discovered our true identity as the begotten of God. The grateful recognition of this is necessarily humble, like Mary's Magnificat. By no means did Mary deny her worth in a false humility. Rather, the thanksgiving and glory she rendered to God was all the richer because she esteemed herself so highly, appreciating to the full all that God had done for her. "He who is mighty has done great things for me, and holy is his name!" (Lk. 1:49).

How far from this is the false humility which refuses to aspire to great holiness and intimacy with God, even though God has come so close to us through Mary!

And how far from this is the self-pity and discouragement which looks only at life's hardships, growing sad over the cost of divine sonship! Self-pity is really a refusal to love oneself as one should, it is a false humility, a sinful self-depreciation, a failure to value self as one called by God to great things and to heroism in laboring for them.

Moreover, to be a prodigal son who is repentant is also to have the joy of honoring God as our Father. In confessing his sins, the Christian is at the same time confessing his joy in his compassionate Father.

Self-Esteem and Esteem for God

Anyone who is unmoved by the thought that we are called to be sons of God and to live in communion with him not only fails in self-esteem but seemingly has little esteem for

God, little understanding of his glorious majesty and infinite lovableness, little appreciation of his love for us and of
the joy of loving him. Lack of interest in prayerful communion with God would seem to indicate that one has not
experienced God's love for him, that one has not tasted that
the Lord is good (Ps. 34:8).

To acquire this taste for the presence of God, this desire
to live in communion with him, one must learn to honor
God for what he is in himself, and not merely for what we
expect him to give us; one must spend time and effort in
prayerful adoration of his majesty simply because he is lovable and adorable, and not merely because we want him to do
something for us. The psalmists were ever praising and
thanking God for what he is in himself and for all his
wonderful works which reveal what he is. (Cf. Ps. 145.)

The more one learns to esteem God sheerly for what he is,
the more one learns to esteem oneself in amazed wonderment
at the divine love which could create us and be bothered
with us. "What is man that thou art mindful of him, and
the son of man that thou dost care for him? Man is like a
breath, his days are like a passing shadow. Yet thou hast
made him little less than God, and dost crown him with
glory and honor" (combining Psalms 144:3–4 and 8:4–5).
Just to be loved by God bestows indescribable value and
dignity upon us.

The self-esteem resulting from this insight into the infinite divine love and majesty, we said, is deeply humble and
grateful. Having such self-esteem, one cannot possibly be
discouraged at one's creaturely helplessness and nothingness,
but only enraptured with the divine love which could create
and redeem us. God's love for us awakens in us a sense of
responsibility to that love, love's obligation to become what

that love expects of us. And one cannot fail to give honor to the love which so loves us, one cannot help rejoicing that God is God.

To fail to live in adoration of God and in communion with him is to fail in proper self-esteem. It is a narrow pride indeed and a sinful self-depreciation which thinks that happiness can be found only in self, or merely in the collective perfection of the human group or community with which one proudly identifies self. This is the contemporary sin of closed humanism, which glories only in man. It is a sort of idolatry of man.

The highest form of self-esteem, then, is the conviction that God desires communion with us; the noblest form of self-love is the continuing effort to enter into this communion. We hold ourselves at our true worth only when we grant God his loving desire to dwell among us. We sell ourselves too cheaply if we do not seek prayerful communion with him.

And we sell God too cheaply if we do not adore him as he deserves. We dishonor his creative love and his Fatherhood if we do not pay fitting attention to that love and live ever in openness to receive what his love wills to accomplish in us, thereby bestowing upon us an ever-increasing dignity and worth. This attitude of attentiveness to God, this openness to his love, this loving response to his invitation, is prayer.

We must not let ourselves deserve the condemnation pronounced by St. Paul upon the pagan world of his times: "Although they knew God they did not honor him as God or give thanks to him" (Rom. 1:21). In consequence, they destroyed their own dignity, falling into the worst kinds of degradation (Rom. 1:21–32).

Self-Esteem and Love of Neighbor

We said that love of self is presupposed to love of neighbor:
"Love your neighbor as yourself." One who does not love
self, one who has little self-respect, finds it difficult to love
and respect anyone else.

And since self-esteem is based on the consciousness of another's esteem for us, one needs to be loved before he can
love others, he needs to acquire a sense of his self-worth if
he is to be able to love his fellowman. Only in a climate of
love can a person learn to love. An unloved child is unable
to love. For one dares to love, one risks giving himself in
love, only when he has some sense of his personal worth,
some reason to expect that his love will be accepted. If he
gives his love and it is rejected, if he is repeatedly hurt by
such rejection, his self-esteem shrivels, he draws back into
his shell and loves no more, his power to love shrinks.

But the more he experiences someone's deep love for him,
and the deeper his consequent self-esteem, the more he is
able to love not only those who love him but many others as
well.

Were these psychological truths applicable also to the
human heart of Jesus? If only a heart that is loved can love,
and if Jesus the man was able to love all mankind with an
all-embracing love transcending all human limitations, it
could only be because the human heart of Jesus experienced
someone's infinite love for him. And indeed he tells us that
he has experienced such love: "As the Father has loved me,
I also have loved you. Remain in my love . . . just as I . . .
remain in his love" (Jn. 15:9–10).

Because Jesus remained in his Father's love, he could continue to love us even when we rejected his love. "He came

unto his own, and his own received him not" (Jn. 1:11). They cried, "Away with him, crucify him" (Jn. 19:15). If his love had been only human, and if he had never experienced any love except human love, could his love have survived this rejection, could he have continued to love?

He did continue to love those who rejected him. "Father, forgive them for they know not what they do" (Lk. 23:34). And he explains to his disciples why he can continue to love when even they abandon him. It is because the Father continues to love him, and he abides in his Father's love. "The hour is coming, indeed it has come, when you will be scattered, every man to his home, and will leave me alone; yet I am not alone, for the Father is with me" (Jn. 16:32–33).

The more anyone has experienced the Father's love for him, and the deeper his self-esteem as a child of God's love, the more he can love his fellowmen and the more universally his love extends. Indeed, only the experience of God's fatherly love enables us to love all men without exception. Jesus implies this when he says that pagans love those who love them, but the children of the heavenly Father love even those who hate them (Mt. 5:47–48). Indeed, only this universal love is the proof that we are sons of the Most High, children of his love (Mt. 5:45). Only the experience of God's compassionate love for us enables us to continue to love even our enemies.

Communion with God and Love of Neighbor

If we are to fulfill the Christian commandment of universal love, then, it is essential that we daily deepen our experience of our heavenly Father's love for us. Regular prayerful communion with the Father is of prime importance if we are to

succeed in persistent love of neighbor. Our failure to love
our fellowmen is due in no small part to our failure to live
in close communion with God, just as communion with God
is hindered by our shortcomings in the love of neighbor.

Just as authentic self-esteem, resulting from our apprecia-
tion of God's boundless love for us, destroys all pride and
rebellion toward God—whom we see not as a threat to our
freedom and personality but as its fulfillment—so too our
self-esteem destroys pride in regard to our fellowman. A
neighbor is no longer seen as a threat to our personal worth,
for the unshakable basis of our self-esteem is our experience
of the Father's undying love for us. Therefore, we need not
seek false grounds to give ourselves a sense of self-worth. We
do not try to bolster up our ego by depreciating a fellowman, or by seeking dominion over him, or by striving for
wealth or power, or even for honest accomplishments for their
own sake alone. We strive to accomplish worthwhile things
only to please our heavenly Father and to help our fellowman, not to lord it over him. And hence our fellowman, who
can so easily surpass us in power and fame and wealth and
human accomplishments, is no longer seen as a threat to our
self-worth. Our self-esteem is solidly grounded in God's love
for us.

Seeing both ourself and others as created and redeemed to
be sons of God, seeing that there is room for all of us in the
boundless love of the heavenly Father, we desire only to
bring our neighbors to the same dignity we ourselves enjoy;
we desire to help them to the self-esteem which expresses
itself in living true to their dignity as sons of God; we desire
to bring all men into communion with God, so that they too
may experience God as their Father and themselves as sons
of the Father. This is the authentic love of neighbor com-

manded in the Scriptures: "You shall love your neighbor as yourself." This is to value him as a person, a son of God destined for personal communion with the Father and with his brothers in Christ.

To love our neighbor in this way presupposes that we love ourselves in this way. Only one who has deeply experienced God's love for him can be very enthusiastic about helping a neighbor to an experience of this same love. Intimate communion with God is therefore essential for authentic Christian self-love and for Christian love of neighbor.

Thus a spirituality which attaches great importance to prayer, to communion with God, is by no means selfish. It is a fulfilling of the command to love self, to esteem self as one called to be a son in communion with his heavenly Father. To refuse this invitation to divine intimacy is a dishonoring of the divine love which calls. The lack of appreciation of one's own divine sonship hardly fits one to esteem a neighbor as a son of God, and deprives one of the power to lead him to the Father.

One cannot, then, love a neighbor as oneself in the fullest meaning of that command if one does not esteem oneself highly as a son of God's love. If love of neighbor strives above all else to bring him into communion with God, this love will be successful in this endeavor only to the extent that we ourselves are in communion with God.

The "as yourself" in the command "love your neighbor" implies that one's primary responsibility is one's esteem for oneself as a close friend of God, a self-esteem which effectively nurtures this communion. This personal holiness, rooted in one's intimate communion with God, grows in love's interpersonal relationships, for love of God needs to be expressed in love of neighbor. Love, and hence holiness, is brought to its highest perfection, of course, in intimate communion with God in faith, hope and love, as God communicates himself ever more fully to the one who loves him.

A Virtuous Circle

The love of God, of self, and of neighbor is thus a virtuous circle, a circular movement spiraling ever higher. They who love God deeply, experiencing this love for them, respond to that love by loving their neighbors with the divine love they have received, desiring to bring them also into the same experience of God's love. Thus they give them the sense of being loved divinely, so that they too can turn to God in love, and, experiencing his love more deeply and personally, can then love others ever more divinely, and, in the very loving of neighbor, experience God's love all the more.

To love self authentically, in the Christian way, is to love God above all things. And to love your neighbor authentically, in the Christian way, is to desire to bring him to love God above all things.

To love God authentically is to love him as Father and Friend. To love him as Friend is to live in communion with him. To love neighbor as self is to labor to bring him into this same communion with the Father. "I shall not call you servants anymore . . . I call you friends, because I have made known to you everything I have learnt from my Father" (Jn. 15:15, j). I have revealed the Father to you, I have given you personal communion with him! "Father, I have made your name known to them, and will continue to make it known, so that the love with which you loved me may be in them, and so that I may be in them" (Jn. 17:26, j).

Hope of Self-Fulfillment

Clearly, then, self-esteem is of great importance in authentic spirituality. Self-esteem, we said, is no mere mental evaluation, no mere wishful thinking. It is true and deep to the extent that it works in our efforts to become all that we ought to be. And since it is a response to someone else's love for us, self-esteem strives to be worthy of that love, strives to please the lover by measuring true to what the lover rightly wants us to be.

Thus self-esteem and the hope of self-fulfillment are not necessarily selfish. They can and should be an expression of love for God and neighbor.

The Quietists of a recent century, seeking to reach a pure love for God, mistakenly considered that hope is a selfish virtue. Charity alone, they maintained, is completely selfless; it is concerned only with the glory of God. Hope, however, is self-centered, for it is a love resulting from one's need, it is a reaching to obtain what is necessary for one's personal fulfillment and one's own happiness. Hope, therefore, would seem to be a virtue only for the less perfect Christian. The "perfect" Christian, they claimed, attains to a pure love of God free of all love of self, a love characterized by complete and holy indifference.

In reply to this, we point out that no virtue is perfect unless it is an embodiment of love, an act in which love finds expression; for example, justice to neighbor should be an expression of love for him. I pay my debts to him, I give him what is his own, because I love him and God.

So, too, hope for one's salvation and personal fulfillment is a perfect virtue when it is an expression of love for God.

Because I love God, I hope to become everything that his love wants me to be. Charity looks upon God precisely as Friend. To please my Friend, whom I love and who loves me, I hope for my personal fulfillment, I labor for it with confidence under God. To please my Friend, I open myself in hope for all that he wants to give me. Because I love him I trust his love, which will accomplish in me, through my faithfulness to his call, the purposes of his divine love.

Such is the spirituality of self-love and personal fulfillment. For love of God and for the manifestation of his glory, I hope to be, I will to be, all that he wants me to be.

My vocation from God is the basic norm of my authentic personal fulfillment. Only through responsible fidelity to this call can I attain it.

Only through this personal fulfillment can I make my full contribution to my fellowmen and to the Christian community. Community becomes the richer the more responsibly each member becomes what he ought to be.

Christian spirituality is thus a spirituality of being authentic, of being yourself—your true self as determined by God's call—for God's sake and for neighbor.

Part Two

THE GENESIS AND DEFINITION
OF SPIRITUALITY

6

PRAYER AND CONSCIENCE: FASHIONERS OF SPIRITUALITY

Prayer: Existential and Experiential

Prayer and conscience, we have seen, begin as a quest and a questioning. They spring forth from our very being, from the neediness of that being.

When authentic, prayer and conscience are existential, completely in touch with reality—they are rooted in existence and they are fashioners of existence, directing it toward fulfillment.

And they are experiential. For, insofar as they are a search for meaning, prayer and conscience are a process in which a man comes to understand himself in relationship to God, through the interpretation of his religious experience.

In his search for meaning and fulfillment, man undergoes a twofold experience, negative and positive—negative, the experience of need, giving rise to questions, problems, mysteries to be solved; and positive, the experience of the initiatives of God's love, working in him through the Holy Spirit. God, who created man with a neediness so that he himself might be its fulfillment, turns in love to his needy creature to bring to fulfillment what he himself has begun. Through his Holy Spirit, he speaks to each man interior "words" of grace; for sooner or later, "the true light enlightens every man" (Jn. 1:9), offering him friendship and communion.

In interpreting these experiences of need and of grace, man discovers certain ontological relationships which exist between himself and God, and between his social group and God, relationships which are built into the very being of things. Experiencing his poverty, for example, he recognizes his relationship of creature to Creator, of needy one to the Source of all that he needs, of beneficiary to Benefactor, of servant to Lord. He experiences these relationships both as individual and as a group.

And in his experience of God's interior word of grace, he discovers his relationships of sinner to Saviour, of son to Father, of friend to Friend.

Spirituality: a Dynamic Structuring of Personality and Life

When one recognizes these various relationships and accepts them from the heart, and structures his life and personality accordingly, then he has a spirituality. Not only an individual but a group can develop a spirituality in this way; and indeed an individual develops his spirituality only in his group.

One's spirituality is the way one stands with God, it is the unified complex of one's relationships with him, it is what one *is* in relationship with God. Or better, it is *who* one is in relationship with him. For spirituality consists in dynamic personal relationships with God. They are personal because they proceed from mind and heart, from knowledge and willingness; and they are dynamic because they are expressed in the human action in which one achieves interpersonal communion with God.

By human action we do not mean mere external activity. Truly human action can be entirely interior, in mind and heart. A human action is one which proceeds from deliberate choice, from will enlightened by intellect.

We exist in dynamic relationship with God through human action—for example, through freely chosen acts of faith, hope, love, religion or service of our fellowmen as child of God. Spirituality is thus a living personal relationship with God. The lesser creatures, such as trees and stones, have merely an ontological relation with God; in their very being they are dependent upon him as creature upon Creator. But this is not a personal relationship, because the dependence is not known and not loved. But when man acknowledges his various ontological relationships with God, when he "interiorizes" them by recognizing them with his mind and embracing them with his heart, he makes these relationships personal, he acts as a person in understanding and accepting them and in freely and responsibly directing his life according to them.

As personal, his relationships are the response of his human person to the divine Persons. Such relationships are at least an initial communion with God, paving the way for an ever deeper interpersonal communion and unity with him.

The relationships discovered in prayer and conscience become incarnate in life when by free and responsible choice one lives according to them. Such a life, living the relationships willingly accepted in prayer, becomes a fullness of prayer.

The relationships become incarnate, too, in the structure of one's personality. Discovered, accepted, deepened in prayer and conscience, they become continuing existential attitudes of one's person, they are built into one's personality.

Spirituality as Stance and as Action

This structuring of one's personality in interpersonal relationships with God is spirituality as a permanent quality of one's existence. It is a dynamic stance from which springs spirituality in action. Because mature conscience is a dynamic, positive search for the right action, the spirituality fashioned by it is dynamic, ever alive in living relationships with God, in human action which is a response to the word of his will and the word of his grace, and which is therefore a true communion with the Lord God. Right relationships with God and true communion with him are possible, of course, only in the Holy Spirit.

Spirituality as a structuring of one's personality becomes firmer and more permanent as the relationships are deepened and purified in continuing prayer and functioning of right conscience, and in action in accord with the prayer and conscience.

Social Spirituality

Spirituality must be structured not only into the individual's personality and life and action but also into the attitudes and life and action of the human society in which he lives. Man's relationships with God cannot possibly be independent of his relationships with his fellowmen.

Though spiritual men have always known this, it has been brought home to us only too painfully by modern man's psychological inability to find God in human society. Modern man's world is so organized around man himself, as its center and goal, that God can scarcely be found in it. Self-centered man has lost his ability to know God, because he has ceased to acknowledge his dependence on God's loving kindness.

All of this, of course, is the result of sin. The effect of sin is to close man to God. Sin alienates him both from God and from his fellowmen. It destroys his power to love. It shuts him off from others, so that he no longer believes that love is possible. The more widespread are the effects of sin, the less man experiences love, and the less he can believe in a God who is love. When sin is deeply structured into human society, it becomes increasingly difficult to find God in that society.

It is clear, then, that a spirituality of right relationships with God and our fellowmen needs to be structured into human culture and social life. Vatican II puts much of the blame for contemporary atheism upon the failure of Christians to build their spirituality into the totality of their daily human relationships. "Believers can have more than a little to do with the birth of atheism. To the extent that they . . . are deficient in their religious, moral or social life, they must be said to conceal rather than to reveal the authentic face of God and religion . . ." (*GS* 19). "The remedy which must be applied to atheism is to be sought . . . in the integral life of the Church and her members. . . . This faith needs to prove its fruitfulness by penetrating the believer's entire life, including its worldly dimensions, and by activating him toward justice and love, especially regarding the needy. What most reveals the presence of God, however, is the brotherly charity of the faithful . . ."(*GS* 21).

Spirituality, then, is no mere private personal matter. To be authentic, spirituality must be incarnate in our whole life and action in community with our fellowmen, it must be incarnate in the culture of the times. If conscience, recognizing and accepting relationships with God, fashions spirituality, it must labor to refashion all of human society into right relationships with God and men. It is more necessary than ever that no one be content with a merely individualistic morality and spirituality (*GS* 30).

Ecclesial Spirituality

Authentic spirituality, we said, springs from man's experience of his needs, and his experience of God's Spirit working in him.

But man experiences his need for his fellowmen as deeply as his need for God. His experience of neediness, of emptiness, is an experience of loneliness. For it is a need for persons, for personal relationships, for communion with others. And ultimately, at its most profound level, it is a need for communion with God in community with his fellowmen.

And his experience of the Spirit working in him can be rightly interpreted only with the help of the community of men with which he lives, for man comes to self-awareness only in community. It is essential, therefore, that the community experience of the Spirit of God be manifest in the whole structuring of the community life in relationships of justice and love.

Spirituality, then, must not be merely a private matter. It must be a dynamic, corporate, social affair. Authentic Christian spirituality is always ecclesial. The Christian fellowship is a communion with God in Christ, in fellowship with the whole People of God (1 Jn. 1:1–4).

Anthropological Spirituality

Since spirituality is the structuring of one's personal and social life in right relationships with God, we can say that authentic spirituality is anthropological. That is, spirituality is *man's* relationship with God in union with his fellowmen, it is mankind's participation in God's own life.

It is necessary to highlight the anthropological aspect of spirituality these days, because modern man is intensely interested in man. Marxism and other forms of atheistic humanism are totally centered in man. They are committed to man and to nothing else. But Christianity is also committed to man; to man, however, *as son of God*. To make Christianity's genuine concern for man clear to our contemporaries, Christian spirituality needs to be proposed in anthropological, incarnational terms, and especially in terms of community. For this reason, in our next section we shall present Christ as the authentic man, and therefore the criterion of all authentic spirituality.

7

THE NEED FOR A CRITERION
OF SPIRITUALITY

Authentic and Inauthentic Spirituality

The term "spirituality" embraces all the stages of inchoate as well as perfected spirituality, natural as well as supernatural, with their varying degrees of understanding and willingness, of authenticity and inauthenticity. For a man's understanding of the reality of himself in relationship with God can be imperfect, and so his acceptance of it will not be fully enlightened; or his understanding can be erroneous and his acceptance misguided; or instead of acceptance there can be rejection; and so on. Even the rejection is a "spirituality" in the broad sense of the word; that is, it is a stance or existential attitude toward God; thus atheism is a kind of "spirituality."

Thus one's spirituality, one's existential personal relationships with God, can be more or less perfect or imperfect, explicit or implicit; they can be right or wrong, authentic or inauthentic, or, as the Scriptures would put it, righteous or unrighteous.

One thing is sure: to the extent that his understanding and acceptance of his relationships with God are true and right, man's attitudes toward God "reflect a ray of that Truth which enlightens all men" (*NA* 2); and indeed, his relationships may already be a response to an interior personal word of grace from that Word who is God. For all righteousness, we shall see, is a response to God's call for friendship and communion with men. "Abraham believed the Lord; and he reckoned it to him as righteousness" (Gen. 15:6).

Because of these varying degrees of rightness and explicitness in man's relationships with God, because of the need of purifying and deepening them, spirituality must be subjected to a continuing refinement and purification. Therefore, a criterion of spirituality is needed. The very fact that we speak of such a thing as authentic spirituality reveals the need for a criterion for judging this authenticity.

To be "authentic" is to be true to one's self, it is to be what one ought to be. But the criterion of authenticity can never be merely one's self alone, or merely one's own experience. For one can be "a self," a person, only in relationship with other persons. And one can come to self-understanding, one can rightly interpret his experience of himself and of reality and of the Holy Spirit, only with the help of his fellowmen, only in interaction with them. In other words, self-understanding can come about only within a frame of reference, only in relationship with the reality of the world of people and things about us. And one's self-understanding as a Christian can come to maturity only within the Christian community, the Church.

Borrowing and Rejecting Spirituality

At first, a person adopts the attitudes of the people among whom he lives, and therefore their attitudes toward God, their spirituality. But if these borrowed attitudes are to become fully personal and truly his own, then he has to interiorize them by understanding their values with his intelligence, and accepting them as good with his will.

If a person rejects the spirituality of those among whom he lives, it may be for any of a number of reasons.

First, and perhaps most commonly, he finds the spirituality difficult to live, though he grasps its value; and shirking the challenge and responsibility of living it, he rationalizes— that is, he finds reasons to justify his shirking of his responsibilities, explaining away the values, gradually blinding himself to them. And, of course, he will pass on to others this blindness and the false attitudes which it entails. Such blindness and false attitudes make it increasingly difficult for him to accept an authentic spirituality, and he cannot live in openness to deep personal relationships with God. "Their very minds and consciences are corrupted. They profess to know God, but they deny him by their deeds" (Tit. 1:15–16; cf. Rom. 1:18–32).

Even when such a man accepts the values of spirituality in theory, if he does not put them into practice, justifying his failure by rationalization, he acquires a blindness, a self-deception, in which he does not realize the discrepancy between his theory and his practice. People younger than he, who are just beginning to come to spiritual awareness, often detect this discrepancy, and they are likely enough to reject the spiritual theory he professes, right though it may be in itself. This is a second reason why spiritualities are rejected.

Thirdly, a person may reject the spirituality of those about him because it does not seem to correspond to his own experience of his needs or to his experience of the grace of the Holy Spirit. He does not want a "prefabricated" spirituality imposed upon him which seems to be out of touch with life as he knows it.

For he cannot really be "authentic" or true to himself in accepting the spirituality of the people with whom he lives, he cannot interiorize their values, embracing them in understanding and love, unless he can see how these values or attitudes correspond to the reality he experiences and give meaning to it. How often the spiritual theories and attitudes of the people with whom he lives do not jibe with what is actually happening in his world of experience. And so he rejects their spirituality, even though it is beautifully worked out in theory in great detail, and may once have been for some people a wholly adequate interpretation of life in relationship with God. He rejects it as a dead spirituality. For the society which presents this theory to him, though it professes to live by it, has not really been living it to the full and this, no doubt, because of the sort of rationalization and blindness of which we spoke above, or because of negligence of one sort or other.

Spirituality: Incarnate in the Culture of the Times and the Place

When our spirituality is not being lived to the full, it gets out of touch with reality. For spirituality is not a mere theory or theology divorced from life. It is a way of life effectively put into daily practice; it is one's relationships with God expressed or incarnate in the actual living of life;

it is a complex of dynamic living relationships with God; it is the totality of life in vital communion with God.

Life, however, is dynamic and ever developing; it expresses itself in ever changing cultures and civilizations, as man develops and uses, in ever differing ways, the world over which God has given him dominion.

Therefore, too, man's relationships with God, as lived and expressed in the totality of life, have to be embodied in the life and culture of the times; they have to be lived and expressed in a way which is completely in touch with the milieu of men and civilization in which he lives, for, as we said, spirituality is not something apart from life; it is life itself in right relationship with God. One must live his relationships with God in all of daily life, in the midst of the human lives and civilization in which he finds himself. A man's spirituality must therefore be incarnate in the culture of his times and of his country; otherwise it is inauthentic and is not viable. An eighteenth-century French way of living the spiritual life, for example, is inauthentic for late-twentieth-century America. By no means does this mean that we in our times cannot learn from the spiritual writers of the past. But we do need to know how to distinguish the invariable essentials of spirituality of which they spoke from the changing elements in which they embodied them in the life of their times.

Some of the troubles in the religious life in America can be traced to the effort to live an alien spirituality, a spirituality which is not embodied in the right and good elements of American culture. For instance, physical penances which perhaps were attractive and helpful to the austere Spanish temperament in the sixteenth century in cloistered life are neither appealing nor necessary, and may even be harmful, in the twentieth-century community of teaching brothers or sisters. Or, a rigid, invariable schedule, ideal perhaps for all religious in the leisurely days of the oxcart, could hamper the spiritual life of a twentieth-century religious who is impelled by God's grace to be alive to the thinking and needs of his contemporaries and to be available to them at all times.[6]

A truly vital, alert spirituality, one which is really lived to the full in every detail of daily life, will be dynamic, up-to-date, expressing itself in forms true to the times and the place. This is not to say that it accepts everything in the culture in whose midst it lives. In fact, it has to fashion or refashion that culture in keeping with the Gospel of Christ. Culture itself needs to be given an authentic spirituality.

Twofold Criterion of Spirituality

For there is a twofold criterion of spirituality to be applied —the times and the Gospel. In fashioning one's spirituality, one must be true to life and reality as one experiences it, but to this life as judged, and if need be corrected, according to the Gospel.

A spirituality which is out of touch with the times and our culture, even though it seems to contain all the authentic Gospel elements, will be rejected by more and more young people, for it seems untrue to life as they experience it, and therefore they are right in judging it inauthentic. A spirituality which is out of touch with our culture is indeed out of touch with our fellowmen in their daily life. To the extent

[6] On the need of embodying one's spirituality in the culture of the times and of the place, see, for example, Stafford Poole, "Americanizing American Religious Life," *America*, March 15, 1969, p. 297.

that one is not in right relationship with his fellowmen, he is not fully right with God. One is justified, then, in rejecting a so-called traditional spirituality to the extent that it is out of touch with the culture of the times.

On the other hand, one rightly rejects a culture to the extent that it is not in right relationship with God.

Needed: a Criterion of Culture

In this second case, it is not the totality of the culture which is to be rejected, and in the first case it is not the totality of the spirituality which is to be rejected. It is rather a case of correcting and purifying the culture and the spirituality, retaining the authentic values of each.

Hence again we see the necessity of a criterion of authenticity, one which will reveal the true values both of culture and of spirituality. In the concrete, spirituality and culture are the one same way of life. Spirituality is the way of life in its relationship with God. Hence the criterion we need must simultaneously reveal the authentic values of life as culture and of life as spirituality, life as secular and life as religious.

In adapting our spirituality to our culture, we have to be careful not to borrow blindly those elements of the culture which stem from man's perverse rationalization of any conduct which is not in right relationship with God, the source of all true values. Speaking of the highly prized values of contemporary culture, Vatican II declares: "Insofar as they stem from endowments conferred by God on man, these values are exceedingly good. Yet they are often wrenched from their rightful function by the taint in man's heart, and hence stand in need of purification" (GS 11). These values must therefore be assessed in the light of faith according to the criterion of the Gospel, the plan revealed by God, whose Spirit fills the earth (*ibid.*).

Being "relevant" to the times, therefore, does not mean being exactly like the times in every imaginable way. Indeed, precisely as witness, the Christian is most relevant to his times when he is somehow different; that is, when he brings to his times those elements of authentic spirituality which the times may be lacking. That is what a witness is: one whose life raises questions in the minds of others because it is different from theirs; different not necessarily in cultural accidentals but in the deep-down meaning which he gives to his life. His different life alerts others to truths which they may have failed to grasp and live. It is a reproach to the falsehood of ungodly and unchristian elements in customs and culture.

In witnessing to certain things—for instance, to prayer and contemplation—a man of the Spirit may be accused of being irrelevant to the secularism of the times, but in fact he is most relevant in bringing to his times something which is sorely needed.

His task is to live his spirituality in such a way that it will shine forth as a convincing answer to the needs of the times. He has to embody his authentic spirituality in the good and acceptable elements of his culture in such a way that his contemporaries see that his life in the Spirit is not the destruction but the perfection of "whatever is true, whatever is honorable, whatever is just, whatever is pure, whatever is lovely, whatever is gracious," excellent, worthy of praise (Phil. 4:8) in the culture of the times.

If he is accused of being irrelevant when he witnesses to certain invariables of Christian spirituality which are rejected by his times, he must have the courage of his convictions and be "irrelevant" and therefore relevant in bringing his times something they need.

Not only must the objective values of a culture and of a spirituality be judged in the light of the Holy Spirit according to the Gospel, but also the subjective attitudes of the one who judges them. For when one rejects either the spirituality or the culture of those among whom he lives, he must be sure of his motivation. Does he reject it because it is opposed to his experience of God's grace and because it is truly out of touch with the times and inadequate to his experienced needs, or does he reject it because it is opposed to his selfishness?

Neither he himself nor his cultural milieu is the fully adequate criterion of authentic spirituality. For just as he himself can misinterpret both his experience of his needs and his experience of grace, just as he himself can rationalize himself into a warped interpretation of self and of life, so can a whole group of men, or a whole civilization, do the same.

Hence, the criterion of authentic culture and spirituality is something beyond the individual and something beyond the community of men. It is the word of God. Prayer and conscience, in building spirituality, must be guided by this word.

8

WORD AND SPIRIT:
CRITERIA OF SPIRITUALITY

Through response to the word of God in faith and fidelity, man comes to righteousness. Righteousness is the scriptural term for authentic spirituality. "Righteousness" is sometimes translated "justice"; and the "righteous man" is called "the just man," the man who is "right," who is what he ought to be.

I. RIGHTEOUSNESS: AUTHENTIC SPIRITUALITY

Spirituality, we said, is a living, personal relationship with God. Righteousness, whether between man and man or man and God, is a term of relationship. "Thus a man is called righteous who conducts himself properly with reference to an existing communal relationship, who, therefore, does justice to the claims which this communal relationship makes on him."[7]

Righteousness is the effective rendering of justice. "Justice is no abstract thing, but denotes the rights and duties of each party arising out of the particular relationship of fellowship in which they find themselves. . . . The task of righteousness is to render effective in the proper way this justice and the claims which it implies, so that the good of all those united in the one community of law may be safeguarded."[8]

Righteousness is thus the behavior which corresponds to, or is true to, the claims arising out of a relationship or communion among persons. It is no mere measuring true to some pre-set, rigid, invariable standard of conduct. It is above all a living personal relationship in which one's conduct is regulated by whatever the relationship calls for in the circumstances and considering the condition of the persons.

As rightness in personal relationships, full righteousness is obviously built upon reverence for others as persons. It requires an alert response to the claims, the needs, the legitimate desires of the other person in each and every situation, so that fellowship and communion will be maintained. Thus in all its fullness, scriptural righteousness is ultimately a synonym for true love, love in action, the specific kind of action called for by the condition of the persons involved and by the situation in which they find themselves. Thus, if one person is in need and the other is able to help, righteousness—the right thing to do, the action called for in the situa-

[7] G. von Rad, *Genesis* (Philadelphia: Westminster, 1961), p. 180.

[8] W. Eichrodt, *Theology of the Old Testament* (Philadelphia: Westminster, 1961), p. 241.

tion—is for the person who can do so to help the one in need. Righteousness is thus dynamic; it is no mere state of being but is a living relationship or fellowship expressed in fitting action.

Indeed, according to the psalmist, help to the needy is the overflowing fullness of justice: the righteous man "is generous and merciful and just. It is well with the man who deals generously and lends, who conducts his affairs with justice; for the righteous will never be moved" (Ps. 112:5–6). Thus generosity and justice are both characteristics of righteousness, both are the right thing to do in one's relationships with others, depending upon the circumstances. Care for the poor is particularly characteristic of the righteous man: "He has distributed freely, he has given to the poor; his righteousness endures forever" (*ibid.,* 9).

Righteousness, love in action, is thus the sum total of right relationships among persons living in communion. There is no love without justice. Indeed, for St. John, righteousness and love of neighbor become almost synonyms: "Whoever is not just" (whoever does not *"do* righteousness") "is not of God, nor is he just who does not love his brother" (I Jn. 3:10, c). Thus we see the truth of St. Paul's claim that love is the fullness of the law, the law which regulates right relationships between man and man, and man and God (Rom. 13:8–10). Love must express itself in the justice called for by the commandments; love does not exist unless it is expressed in right and just relationships. Clearly, rightness with God, authentic spirituality, includes rightness with fellowmen.

Righteousness is always salvific, *justitia salutifera,* "health-bringing," for it preserves the health and welfare of the community, it promotes the common good.

Righteousness and Faith in the Word of God

Because of God's covenant with his people, a communal relationship or fellowship exists between him and them. Consequently, righteousness is a characteristic of both God and man in their mutual relationships.

God is ever right and just in his dealings with his people, everything he does in regard to them is for the purpose of perfecting his communion with them. His word and will to which his people must respond in the covenant relationship is ever salvific, *salutifera,* salvation-bringing; it is always a word and will of love.

But since communion is a mutual relationship, righteousness is also called for on the part of man. Righteousness, we said, requires reverence for the other person, it is ever attentive to his welfare and just wishes, it responds as the situation requires. Righteousness in relationship to God also is basically a reverence for him and therefore for his word, which is received in faith.

The fundamental element in man's righteousness, then, is the faith in which he commits himself totally to God in openness to his friendship, in response to his word. Thus, Abraham "believed the Lord; and he reckoned it to him as righteousness" (Gen. 15:6).

And righteousness is ever characterized by an undying loyalty to God and fidelity to the word of the covenant thus established. This faithfulness is expressed in loving action in accord with God's word and saving will. Because Abraham remained faithful in every test to which his faith was put, he was called "the friend of God." "Remember how our father Abraham was tempted, and being proved by many tribulations, was made the friend of God" (Judith 8:22, d).

Hence righteousness is always a response to God's word calling for communion with man. The criterion of spirituality is thus the word of the Lord which expresses his salvific will, his will to have men as his sons and friends.

The word of the Lord is not merely the scriptural word, but above all an interior personal word of grace, to which each one's conscience must be ever alert, to which he must be ever surrendered in living faith. Faith, as total commitment to the personal call of God, is a surrender of self to the purposes of his love. Righteousness, we said, is no mere measuring true to some invariable standard of conduct. It is above all a dynamic personal relationship with God in which one's conduct is regulated by whatever the relationship calls for in the circumstances, whatever God wills in the situation. Because his begetting love has created and redeemed us, the filial relationship with him always calls for the loving gift of self in return, in faith and absolute trust, a living giving in the daily following of his salvific will.

For the salvation and communion to which he calls us surpasses all human understanding, and one can trust only in his guidance. Hence faith and righteousness is ever an openness to the unexpected, a readiness for anything at all that God's word might ask of us. "By faith Abraham obeyed . . . and went out, not knowing where he was to go" (Heb. 11:8). The Word and Spirit of God lead us we know not where. It is right and just that we be ever surrendered to this Word and Spirit, ever alert to carry out whatever the Lord asks, no matter how disconcerting his will may be.

Spirituality is thus basically this relationship to God in total trust, this constant giving of self to him in hope, for the accomplishment of the purposes of his love.

The New Testament makes clear that righteousness is a

gift of God in Christ Jesus and is accomplished in us by the outpouring of the Holy Spirit into our hearts. Only the Holy Spirit can set man right with God. "Create in me a clean heart, O God, and put a new and right spirit within me. Cast me not away from thy presence, and take not thy holy Spirit from me" (Ps. 51:10–11).

Though righteousness is the biblical term for authentic spirituality, we rightly call it spirituality—life in the Spirit— for true righteousness is possible only in the Spirit.

II. CONSCIENCE AND THE INCARNATE WORD

Man's conscience receives the word of God's will in a variety of ways; for God speaks to us in many different signs which reveal his presence and action in the world and in our personal lives.

And somehow the word he speaks to us is always Christ.

Christ, the Eternal Word, speaks to us chiefly in these ways:

As creator Word he speaks to my conscience through creation itself and through my situation in that creation. Especially the creator Word speaks through human nature, which, through conscience, can know the law of God.

As incarnate and redeeming Word, Christ speaks to my heart in the living Gospel; that is, in everything he himself was and said and did in his life and death and resurrection.

He addresses this Gospel to me in the scriptural record of his saving action, both Old and New Testaments, and in that same Gospel as continued in the life of his mystical body, the Church.

As the Word who is Lord of the world through his resurrection—"the heir of all things, upholding the universe by the word of his power" (Heb. 1:2–3)—Christ speaks to me in the signs of the times, his action in the world today, which reveals to me, in the light of the Holy Spirit, his presence and purpose for the Church, for mankind, and for me personally (*GS* 11).

Especially he speaks to my conscience in my unique daily personal situations, that part of his universal action which is most significant for me personally (and most of all in my relationships with my fellowmen); for nothing escapes the power and wisdom of his providence in ruling the total cosmos and my personal life. True righteousness always responds to the requirements of the situation in which God has placed me.

An enlightened and mature conscience knows how to "hear" God's word speaking in all these signs, for my unique personal word is always within the context of creation and the mystery of redemption in Christ and the Church.

The word spoken to me by my conscience, no matter how it comes to me, is always uniquely my word, it is God's word to me personally. Conscience is the sanctuary where *I* meet the God who awaits me there. The word of conscience is a word of truth, my personal truth, the truth of life for me in my life here and now, the truth of living action, the action which is right and good for me in this particular situation, the action in which I will be what I ought to be, my true self in the making.

The Personal Interior Word of Grace

Though Christ the Word speaks to me personally in all the above-mentioned ways—through creation, salvation history, the Church, his action in the world today, my personal situation—above all and most necessary of all, "the true light that enlightens every man" speaks to me a personal interior word of grace addressed to my heart (Jn. 1:9). "He calls his own sheep by name" (Jn. 10:3).

For none of the other words of God are meaningful to me unless the Word speaks a word of interior vocation to my heart. To that, above all, my conscience must ever be attentive. Without that interior light, everything else is darkness.

Sooner or later, this interior personal call comes to every man (Jn. 1:9). When man follows his conscience and does what is right, a grace of divine light is granted to him, the Word himself comes and dwells in him in the gifts of justifying grace—and everything takes on its true meaning for him, all creation speaks a new language to him, and in this Light he has power to recognize the word of God no matter in what way it may come to him: in nature, in his fellowmen, in the Gospel, in the Person of Christ, in the Church, in every providential situation; though it may take time for him to interpret rightly all these other words of God in the light of the interior word.

But if I reject the interior personal light, either when it is first offered to me or in any later situation, then the "eye" or light in me becomes darkness and I lose the power to see God in the multitude of ways in which he reveals himself to me, I no longer recognize his word when he addresses me. I no longer hear him speaking to me in creation or in my fellowmen or in any other way. For the word of God can be heard only by a heart open to God, one which has not deliberately shut itself to him by a violation of conscience.

We hasten to add that we have described this darkness at its worst. For the darkening of conscience is usually a gradual process; just as the enlightenment of a man who follows his conscience is gradual, as more and more he lets Christ, the indwelling Light, extend his power and guidance to the totality of his life.

Light and Darkness

In an analysis of the biblical doctrine on light and life, darkness and death, and commenting especially on the words of St. John, "In him was life and the life was the light of men" (Jn. 1:4), A. Hulsbosch writes:

> The intelligence is light only when directed to God. Otherwise it is darkness. . . . According to Scripture, there is light only in the man in communion with God. . . . It is possible for man to dowse this light. One goes on thinking and reasoning, but one's heart is darkened. "They became futile in their thinking and their senseless minds were darkened" (Rom. 1:21). . . . It is only for the man who stands open to God that the world is irradiated by light. . . . It is from the orientation to God, which constitutes the essence of man, that all human knowledge derives its worth. Without this light he sees nothing, though he should investigate the whole world with his scientific insight.[9]

We can understand, then, why Vatican II appeals to modern man, so enamored of his science and technology, to develop carefully the faculty of wonder and contemplation, along with a religious and moral sense (*GS* 59).

Ecclesiasticus, which has much to say about conscience and moral freedom,[10] tells us that God gave man a conscience,

---

[9] A. Hulsbosch, *God in Creation and Evolution* (New York: Sheed and Ward, 1956), pp. 59, 81, 84.

[10] For example, Ecclus. 15:11–20.

endowing it with his own "eye." "He gave them a heart to think with . . . he put his own light [literally, 'eye'] in their hearts" (Ecclus. 17:57, j).

The biblical background given by Hulsbosch gives a new impact to our Lord's words: "Your eye is the lamp of your body. When your eye is sound, your whole body is full of light; but when it is not sound, your body is full of darkness. Therefore be careful less the light in you be darkness" (Lk. 11:34–35). "If the light in you is darkness, how great is the darkness!" (Mt. 7:22).

Hulsbosch writes: "Modern philosophy has once more made it clear that human ocular vision is a spiritual act that differs from animal vision as man does from the animal. This intuition of the unity of man was possessed by the Israelites also. They saw the body as the exteriorization of the person, and physical vision as the exteriorization of inward vision. The difference from philosophy is that, in the Bible, exterior seeing only gives light when the inner man is illuminated by communion with God."[11]

St. Catherine of Siena, too, with her usual solid psychology and deep scriptural understanding, saw the unity of nature and grace, of natural intelligence and faith, and knew that man is incomplete and blind without faith. Faith, she says again and again, is the pupil of the eye of the intellect. What one sees with eye and intellect in the world about him loses its divine meaning, its authentic meaning, when man is not in communion with God in faith. He who dowses the light by repeatedly violating his conscience, he who "has resolved against possessing the knowledge of God" (Rom. 1:28, c), becomes blind to the creative Word speaking to him in all things, he can no longer find God in nature or in his fellow-

---

11 Hulsbosch, *op. cit.*, p. 82.

men, and he cannot see Christ. "For everyone who does evil hates the light, and does not come to the light, that his deeds may not be exposed" (Jn. 3:20, c). And so he is "without God in this world" (Eph. 2:12, c). For him, God is dead.

For such a one, life is no longer light, but darkness. Life is no longer a prayer, but a sin. If a man's whole life can be an incarnate prayer, it can also be an incarnate sin. It is not for this or that sinful act that a man is condemned to hell. It is only he whose *life* is sin who is condemned.

Take care, then, of your heart (Prov. 4:23). Only when the Light, who wills to enlighten every man, dwells in it, is it truly the spring of life. Man lives only in response to the Word of God, and not on bread alone.

III. THE WORD OF GOD: JUDGMENT
AND GOSPEL

The Scriptures present the word of God as a judgment pronounced upon men and a call to set themselves right with God. "Come now, let us set things right, says the Lord" (Isa. 1:18, c); "come now, let us reason together, says the Lord" (*ibid.*, rsv).

"For the word of God is living and active, sharper than any two-edged sword . . . discerning the thoughts and intentions of the heart" (Heb. 4:12). Scrutinizing his heart, judging him, the word calls man to task. It condemns what he has made of himself through sin and it manifests what God calls him to be. God's word is thus the criterion of human conduct, the norm of righteousness.

The word always remains in judgment upon man: "The word that I have spoken will condemn him on the last day" if he has not corrected himself in accordance with it, if he has not lived in conformity with it (Jn. 12:48). "And this is the judgment, that the light has come into the world, and men loved darkness rather than light, because their deeds were evil" (Jn. 3:19).

But in the very act of condemning what man has become, the word is a gospel, good news, for it is an invitation to correction, to conversion, to reconciliation with God: "Jesus came into Galilee, preaching the gospel of God and saying, 'The time is fulfilled, and the kingdom of God is at hand; repent, and believe in the gospel' " (Mk. 1:14–15). Repent, be converted to God's word, conform to it, and you will be right with God again, reconciled to him, at peace with him, restored to his friendship.

The word clarifies the conditions for this communion between God and man: "If a man loves me, he will keep my word, and my Father will love him, and we will come to him and make our home with him" (Jn. 14:23).

The very word which condemns unrighteousness is thus a word of hope; for not only is it a call to conversion, to set things right with God, but it is a power to set things right, it brings the grace to do this. "For I am not ashamed of the gospel, for it is the power of God unto salvation to everyone who believes" (Rom. 1:16). Faith in the word brings the grace of justification, the grace by which God sets the sinner right, the grace to live according to the word; the word which is the criterion of man's relationship with God.

The Living Gospel: the Incarnate Word

But man needs more than a set of verbal directions to guide his life. He needs not only to be told what to do but to be shown how to do it. He needs to see the directions embodied in the life of a man. Christ is this embodiment of the word of God, he is the Word Incarnate, the living Gospel, the criterion of human conduct, the revelation of authentic man. As norm of authentic spirituality, he shows a man in right relationship with God.

In fact, only in the Word himself, only in his paschal mystery, can man be right with God. To be an authentic man, a man must enter into the Word's own personal relationships with the Father, he has to be a "son in the Son" (*GS* 22).

The Living Gospel: the Church

And yet, as we have seen, for spirituality to be authentic it has to be embodied in the culture of the times. Christ was the Word Incarnate in his times and culture. How can he be the norm for our times? Somehow he has to be seen incarnate in our contemporary culture.

For we have noted that a man comes to authentic self-understanding only in the community of men, by learning to see himself in his relationships with others. Society is his norm of self-interpretation.

It is essential, therefore, that society itself be in accordance with Christ, the norm for all men. A society has to be a living Gospel, an incarnation of Christ, the Word. And such indeed is the Church, the mystical Body of Christ, the embodiment of the Word in the lives of his members.

The Church is the living Gospel because it is in living continuity with Christ himself, it is a living Gospel which has the power to continue to grow and renew itself and adapt itself to all variations of time and place, the power to express itself in every human culture in every age of history. "By the power of the Gospel, the Holy Spirit keeps the Church ever youthful and perpetually renews her and leads her to perfect union with her Spouse" (*LG* 4).

Tradition: the Living Continuity of the Church's Life

The standard, therefore, for judging, interpreting, correcting and deepening the religious experience of mankind, and any spirituality resulting from the recognition and acceptance of this experience, is the Gospel—not just the written word of the Gospel, but Christ the living Gospel, and Christ the living Gospel as living in his Church. That is, the norm of spirituality is tradition, but tradition not as a collection of verbal statements or discourses or writings about truth, but the very life of the Church as handed on in living continuity with Christ, handed on in the very living of it.

Therefore, contemporary spirituality must be studied and judged and corrected, if need be, in the light of this living tradition. This living tradition was ever being interpreted and expressed by the Fathers and Doctors and theologians of the Church in the past, and therefore a study of their writings and of the history of spirituality is necessary for an authentic contemporary spirituality. The Christian experience is a living continuity going back to the Apostles and Christ, and indeed, back to the very beginnings of divine revelation, and therefore all of this is apropos for a spirituality of our times. It is not enough to study contemporary needs and experiences and trends. These must be interpreted and integrated into the Christian religious experience of the past as expressed in the Scriptures and the traditional theological writings and in Christian history, especially in the lives of the saints.

The "Experienced" Gospel

The norm of spirituality has to be a living Gospel in the sense of an experienced Gospel, one which has been tried and has succeeded in the very living of it, one which has really worked in human life and is so working now, one which is really answering human needs and rightly interpreting and articulating the interior workings of grace in the hearts of all men.

It has to be an experienced, living Gospel which is fully working here and now in today's culture, fully responding to man's contemporary needs and rightly articulating his interior personal call of grace. Such a vital, incarnate spirituality, fully alive to our times and alive in our times, can be accepted by the men of our times. A traditional, fully living spirituality which is being handed on in the very living of it, a dynamic spirituality which is ever young, ever renewing itself in the power of the Holy Spirit, will be accepted by each new generation, for it will respond to their needs, it will correspond to life as they experience it, it will interpret for them the interior graces they are receiving in their hearts. They will not reject it as they would a cut-and-dried spirituality which is out of touch with the times. They will see it as the Gospel in the flesh and blood of our times, as incarnate in the modern way of life, as meaningful in everyday life as they experience it, and so they will heartily accept it.

Witness to the Living Gospel

Hence the insistence of Vatican II on witness to Christ, the showing forth of Christ in contemporary life; specifically, "the witness of a living and mature faith, namely, one trained to see difficulties clearly and to master them" (*GS* 21), solving them in the light of Christ, in the manner of Christ, thus living the life of Christ and revealing him in everyday affairs of life. Indeed this witness is, in a sense, a manifestation of the Holy Trinity. "For it is the function of the Church, led by the Holy Spirit who renews and purifies her ceaselessly, to make God the Father and his Incarnate Son present and in a sense visible" (*GS* 21). Authentic spirituality, we shall see later, is a participation in the very life of the Holy Trinity, and therefore a striking witness to it.

IV. THE HOLY SPIRIT: SUPREME NORM OF SPIRITUALITY

The first and last norm of all spirituality is the interior grace of the Holy Spirit, to whom, above all, one must be ever alert and attentive. Indeed, the Word of God is meaningless to us without the inner light of the Holy Spirit.

As we have noted, however, this interior grace is too big for words, it surpasses human understanding, and can be interpreted and grasped in a human way only with the help of human experience, only in relationship with our fellowmen, only as seen also in its effects in the lives of fellowmen who themselves are a living gospel, a response to God's word and Spirit. We begin to understand what is taking place in ourselves through God's grace when we see more clearly in the lives of others something corresponding to what we are beginning to experience ourselves, something therefore which gives meaning to our own interior graces.

On the other hand, the Gospel as lived by others will be meaningless to us unless the Spirit of God is working in us. Christ, the living Gospel himself, could not be grasped unless his interior grace was working in the hearts of those who saw and heard him: "No one can come to me unless the Father who sent me draw him" (Jn. 6:44). The word of God can penetrate our hearts and influence our lives only under the action of the Holy Spirit.

Thus St. John speaks of an unction received from Jesus which abides in the Christian and teaches him interiorly (1 Jn. 2:21, 27). This unction is the word of God assimilated in faith under the influence of the Holy Spirit. Like a penetrating oil, the Holy Spirit permeates the hearts of men, giving them understanding of the word of God and inspiration to live it.

God's word would not bear fruit if it were not interiorized in this way under the action of the Holy Spirit, whose interior witness gives us peace and certitude that this *is* God's word, along with joy in living it.

Therefore the Spirit himself, even more profoundly than the word of God, is the ultimate criterion of all spirituality. He himself, says St. Augustine, is the New Law: "What else are the divine laws written by God himself on our hearts but the very presence of his Holy Spirit?"[12]

Hence, the cardinal point in all spirituality will ever be: openness to the Spirit, attentiveness to his inspirations. "He will guide you into all the truth" (Jn. 16:13).

---

[12] *De Spiritu et Littera,* ch. 24. See also St. Thomas Aquinas, *Summa Theologica,* Ia—IIae, Q. 106, a. 1.

9

SPIRITUALITY:
LIFE IN THE SPIRIT

We have defined spirituality as the dynamic structuring of
our life and action and personality in right relationships with
God. This can be done only in the Holy Spirit and requires
persistent prayerful attention to his workings in our heart.

Words such as "spirituality" and "spiritual life"—and
therefore spirituality itself—are often rejected by our contemporaries because for them these words carry some un-
fortunate connotations arising from certain inauthentic elements in Christian spirituality as it has been lived here or
there or in this century or that. The fault, however, is not
with the Gospel or with Christianity itself, but with certain
deficient incarnations of the Gospel in human culture.

Therefore we must further define what we mean by spirituality. When we use the terms spiritual and spirituality in
this book, we do not mean them in a Manichean or in a

Platonic sense which sets up an opposition between body and spirit and considers that the spirit is in the body as in a prison. Our contemporaries rightly object to any dualistic anthropology which divides man into opposing parts, and they often react to the word "spirituality" as connoting for them "disembodied spirit," and mortification as hatred of the body, and therefore the destruction of man.

In the biblical view of man, however, and in the authentic Christian tradition,[13] man is a unity, and Christ is the Saviour of the whole man, body and soul.

We use the words "spiritual" and "spirituality" in the biblical sense, especially as found in St. Paul.

In the Scriptures, the opposition is not between body and soul but between flesh and spirit (Gal. 5:17).

Flesh and Spirit

"Flesh" in biblical usage connotes the weak and perishable aspect of man. "All flesh is grass" (Isa. 40:6). Because the messianic, eschatological era is characterized by the sending of the Spirit, St. Paul can use the word "flesh" to signify the old, unredeemed order as opposed to the new order in the Spirit. Thus "flesh" is not simply the body and its passions, but is man—body and soul—in his sinful condition; "flesh" is unredeemed man.

"Flesh"—that is, man without the Spirit of God—is prone to sin and death; in fact, sin so operates in unredeemed man that Paul personified "flesh" as a power of evil, hostile to God (cf. Rom. 8:5-8) and lusting against the spirit (Gal. 5:17).

---

[13] Thomas Aquinas, for example, strongly asserts the unity of man, in reaction to the dualism of the Albigensians, the heresy counteracted by St. Dominic.

If, then, "flesh" means weak and unredeemed man, "spirit" is man possessed by the Spirit of God, it is the dynamic presence of the Spirit of God in a man, it is man's spirit when man is led by the Spirit of God. St. Paul uses the word "spirit" in these various ways. Indeed, the man possessed by the Holy Spirit is called "spirit" ("That which is born of the Spirit is spirit"—Jn. 3:6).

The Man of the Spirit

Or again, he is called the "spiritual man"—*pneumatikos* (1 Cor. 2:15). This would be better translated as "the man of the Spirit," for *pneumatikos* is the whole man—body and soul—who lives by the Spirit and walks in the Spirit (Gal. 5:25). He is the man who possesses the Spirit, or better, is possessed by the Spirit.[14]

Whereas we today speak of "being justified, being in the state of sin, being in the state of grace," ancient Christians expressed the same truths by speaking of "receiving the Spirit, losing the Spirit, having the Holy Spirit."[15] These Christians were more conscious than we are, it seems, of uncreated grace; that is, of God's gift of himself to us that he might dwell in us, that we might possess him. To be in the state of grace is to possess God. "Having the Spirit" really means being sons of God in the Son, crying "Abba!" in the Holy Spirit of adoption. It means participation in the very life of the Holy Trinity.

[14] See *The Jerusalem Bible* on Rom. 7:5; Rom. 5:5; 1 Cor. 15:44. See also L. Bouyer, *Introduction to Spirituality* (Collegeville, Minn.: Liturgical Press, 1961), pp. 126f.

[15] H. Rondet, *The Grace of Christ* (Westminster, Md.: Newman Press, 1966), p. 69.

Christian spirituality, then, is life in the Spirit. The whole man is taken up into this spirituality. The whole man, possessing the Spirit of God, is called "spirit." St. Paul writes, "May your spirit and soul and body be kept sound and blameless at the coming of our Lord Jesus Christ" (1 Thess. 5:23). The whole man is redeemed, sanctified, glorified. By "soul" in this passage, St. Paul does not mean soul in our sense of soul distinct from body, nor soul as the Greeks thought of it, a prisoner which needs to be freed from the body. In biblical thought, soul and body are not two parts of differing nature, they are but aspects or manifestations of one whole man. Soul is the vital aspect of man, it is man as alive. Body is his material aspect. But for St. Paul there is a third aspect—*pneuma,* spirit: "May your body, soul, and spirit be kept sound and blameless."

In the man who does not have the Spirit of God, the combination is "body, soul and mind (*nous*)." Mind is that which directs man as a human being. But spirit is that which directs him as a son of God. When the spirit of God dwells in a man, mind becomes spirit. St. Irenaeus says, "Perfect man is composed of three elements: body, soul, and Spirit." Man is incomplete unless he possesses God within him as in a living temple.

When the soul attaches itself to the Holy Spirit, it is elevated by him; but when it gives in to the body, it falls into worldly desires. Many men do not possess the Spirit who saves and who gives life. These are the ones whom St. Paul calls "flesh and blood" and who will not inherit eternal life (1 Cor. 15:50). . . .

But all they who fear God, and who believe in the coming of his Son, and who by faith establish the spirit of God in their hearts, these merit to be called "spiritual" because they have the

Spirit of the Father, who purifies man and raises him to the life of God. . . .

The weakness of the flesh, absorbed by the Spirit, manifests the power of the Spirit; and the Spirit, absorbing this weakness, possesses the flesh as his heritage (*PG* 7:1144–45).

That is, the Holy Spirit possesses the whole man, body and soul, as one entity. St. Irenaeus thus refutes the dualistic philosophies which considered the soul as a prisoner in the body, from which it must seek release. On the contrary, the flesh itself, when the soul attaches itself to the Holy Spirit, becomes the precious heritage of the Holy Spirit.

"Living man," Irenaeus continues, "is composed of these two elements: the Holy Spirit, and the man possessed by him. He is man by reason of the substance of his flesh, he is living man, thanks to his participation in the Holy Spirit" (*ibid*).

But may we say that every Christian is a man of the Spirit? May one be called "spiritual" from the mere fact that the Person of the Spirit dwells in him? In one sense yes, and in another sense no. For St. Paul, speaking of the man of the Spirit, goes on to scold the Corinthians for being still too carnal, not spiritual enough. "But I, brethren, could not address you as spiritual men, but as men of the flesh, as babes in Christ. . . . You are still of the flesh. For while there is jealousy and strife among you, are you not of the flesh, and behaving like ordinary men?" (1 Cor. 3: 1–3).

Walk in the Spirit!

For though the Holy Spirit dwells in us, we often fail to walk according to the Spirit. Hence St. Paul speaks not only of the "man of the Spirit" (*pneumatikos*) but also of the "natural man" (*psychikos*, 1 Cor. 2:14), who cannot know the things of God. Only in the Spirit can we penetrate the deep things of God (1 Cor. 2:10f). Worse than "natural man" is "sensual" or "carnal man" (*sarkikos*), who is characterized not by fraternal love and unity in the Spirit but by jealousy and strife (1 Cor. 3:1–3).

Once in a public lecture, someone from the audience, implying from the context that mortification is inhuman, asked Father Bernard Haring, "Isn't it true that the more human we are, the more Christian we are?" Father Haring replied that it should be stated the other way round: "The more Christian you are, the more human you will be." For the perfect man, the Christian man, is one who is redeemed by Christ in the Holy Spirit. It is our fallen "carnal" nature, with its selfishness and strife, which is inhuman and in need of continuing redemption. We cannot be fully human unless we are led by the Holy Spirit, and "by the Spirit put to death the deeds of the body" (Rom. 8:13).

Therefore, instead of putting all the emphasis on being human, on being "natural man," we should put the emphasis on being "men of the Spirit," ever open and responsive to the Spirit of God. And he will make us sons and daughters of God who are as truly human and loving and compassionate as Jesus himself.

Hence the frequent exhortations of St. Paul to be faithful to the Spirit, to live true to what we are! "If we live by the Spirit, let us also walk by the Spirit" (Gal. 5:25). "If you live according to the flesh you will die, but if by the Spirit you put to death the deeds of the body you will live. For all who are led by the Spirit of God are the sons of God" (Rom. 8:13–14).

"Walk by the Spirit, and do not gratify the desires of the flesh. For the desires of the flesh are against the Spirit, and the desires of the Spirit are against the flesh; for these are opposed to each other" (Gal. 5:17).

The desires of the Spirit are the desires which he inspires in us. This presupposes God's ardent desire for us. Desiring communion with us, he inspires us by his Spirit to desire communion with him.

"The Spirit which dwells in you covets unto jealousy" (Jas. 4:5, c).

The initiative in all spirituality comes from God who gives us his Spirit. Man can say with great confidence, "Father, give me the Good Spirit!" (Lk. 11:13), knowing that the Father is even more eager to give him than we are to have him; for the spirit of man was made for the Spirit of God. God is exceedingly eager to put his own Spirit into the spirit of man, that man might cry, "Father!"

St. James expresses all this very strikingly when he writes: "He yearns jealously over the spirit which he has made to dwell in us" (Jas. 4:5). This translation spells "spirit" with a small "s" as speaking of man's created spirit. Other translations spell it with a capital "S," referring it to the Holy Spirit.

If we take "spirit" to refer to man's spirit, the passage means that God yearns over the spirit of man which he created in him, ardently desiring his friendship. God yearns for man like a jealous husband for his wife. (St. James has just branded as adulterous those who love the world in preference to the God who loves men so ardently—Jas. 4:4.) So great and intense is the love of God for us that when there is danger that he will lose our love, the Scriptures describe him as jealous. "The Lord your God is a devouring fire, a jealous God" (Deut. 4:24). "Thus says the Lord of hosts: I am jealous for Zion with great jealousy" (Zach. 8:2). The apostle Paul burns with God's own ardent love for his People: "I am jealous for you with a divine jealousy. For I betrothed you to one spouse that I might present you a chaste virgin to Christ" (2 Cor. 11:2, c).

Other translators interpret "spirit" to mean the Holy Spirit: "He yearns jealously over the Spirit which he has put in our hearts" (Goodspeed). That is, God not only yearns for man's spirit to turn to him in love, but jealously preserves in him his Holy Spirit which he has given him, for only in this Holy Spirit can man have this loving union with him.

In another way of translating the passage, God's jealous love is shown to be exceedingly close to man, it is dwelling within him: "The Spirit who dwells in us longs for us even to jealousy" (s); "The Spirit which dwells in you covets unto jealousy" (c). God's yearning for us is so strong that he puts his very jealousy within us in the person of his Spirit who covets us and guards us jealously.

A man who ardently loves God sometimes actually experiences the Holy Spirit within him in this way—as Someone guarding him jealously for God, longing to bring him to his fulfillment as child and spouse of God.

There are various signs of the indwelling Spirit's jealous guardianship of God's chosen ones.

First there is the ardent cry, "Abba, Father!" inspired in man's heart by the Holy Spirit. Then there is the reaching for God, the groping for him "with sighs too deep for words" which are inspired by the Spirit who "intercedes for the saints according to the will of God" (Rom. 8:26–27). God's ardent love for man, poured into his heart in the gift of the Holy Spirit (Rom. 5:5), returns to God in man's love for him in that same Holy Spirit (Rom. 8:15).

Another sign of the Spirit's jealous guardianship of a man's heart is the man's quick flight from evil, his spontaneous turning to God at the very first threat of temptation. A man, for example, who is sincerely seeking God, trying to please him in all things, taking care to turn to God from evil whenever it presents itself, may find himself in a temptation; for instance, looking attentively at an alluringly beautiful woman; but in the very instant a lustful desire is about to begin in him, the Holy Spirit snatches him away, catching him up in an ardent sigh for God, an act of love for God which utterly destroys the temptation and deepens his communion with God.

This sort of jealous guardianship of his heart by the Holy Spirit will be experienced by the man who persistently and perseveringly seeks God in prayer and in conscience, taking care to keep his heart pure, guarding his senses and desires at all times, making the regular effort to lift mind and heart to God, paying the price of intimate friendship with God.

But no matter how hard he strives for this prayer and purity of heart, he remains a weak man—"all flesh is grass" (Isa. 40:6)—and can still fall. The Spirit, however, will jealously keep him safe in danger, because he has taken care to do his part in guarding himself for God.

And even if, perchance, he does fall into sin in his weakness, the jealous Spirit will inspire in him an act of quick and sincere contrition.

*"Draw near to God and he will draw near to
you" (Jas. 4:8)*

Because the "Spirit covets unto jealousy" he is eager and
generous in giving his grace. That seems to be the meaning
of James in adding immediately, "but he gives more grace"
(Jas. 4:6). James then tells on what conditions this grace is
given: "God opposes the proud, but gives grace to the humble. Submit yourselves therefore to God. Resist the devil and
he will flee from you. Draw near to God and he will draw
near to you. Cleanse your hands, you sinners, and purify
your hearts, you men of double mind. . . . Humble yourselves before the Lord and he will exalt you" (Jas. 4:6–10).

Draw near to God and he will draw near to you. The
prompt turning to God in every difficulty, the quick resistance to evil and the humble submission to God, are all signs
that the jealous Spirit is guarding his own. If anyone is seeking God, it is because God is seeking him still more.

Because he loves unto jealousy, he pours out his grace
upon the humble who turn to him. His eager love can be
received only in an eager return of love.

Knowing that God yearns for us with jealousy, we dare to
pray: "Lord, possess me totally. Envelop me completely in
your protecting Spirit, lead me always by his inspirations.
And may he inspire in me your own jealous love for your
People, as he inspired St. Paul. Fill the spirits of men which
you created for your Holy Spirit."

The inspirations of this Spirit are the only adequate norm
of spirituality, which is life in the Spirit.

10

IS SPIRITUALITY ONE OR MANY?

To say, as we did in our preceding chapters, that the word of God and Christ, and the Holy Spirit, are the criteria of spirituality seems to imply that only Christian spirituality is authentic. The question therefore arises: Can there be authentic non-Christian, or even atheistic, spirituality?

This question, in fact, did arise, along with a number of related questions, when the ideas of the preceding two chapters were presented in a lecture to graduate students of theology. One student refused to admit that there has to be a criterion of spirituality. There is no such thing as objective truth, he claimed, and therefore we must allow for pluralism in spirituality as in everything else. Another student objected to the idea that all true spirituality begins with God working in us by his Holy Spirit. He seemed to think that this amounts to saying that spirituality must always begin with prayer, and like so many of our contemporaries he doubted the necessity of prayer, claiming that "being with people" is prayer. Still another student, mistrusting institutionalized religion, rejected the idea that the Church is in some way the criterion of spirituality. For this student, the only authentic norm of spirituality would be "humanity." To be human, she maintained, is to be Christian.

This is true enough if in turn we accept Christ as the norm of authentic humanity, as we shall do in our chapters entitled Authentic Man. The present chapter is a response to these objections.

The Word of God and Non-Christian Spirituality

Can there be authentic non-Christian spirituality? Hans Urs von Balthasar writes: "There is no reason to limit spirituality to the context of Christianity." And he gives a broad definition of spirituality which would apply to anyone's spirituality:

Spirituality may be approximately defined as that basic practical or existential attitude of man which is the consequence of and expression of the way in which he understands his religious or even more generally his ethically committed existence.[16]

This existential attitude may be right or wrong in greater or lesser degree, for his understanding of the ontological reality of the world and himself in relationship to God may

[16] Hans Urs von Balthasar, "The Gospel as Norm and Test of All Spirituality in the Church," *Spirituality in the Church and World,* Concilium IX (New York: Paulist Press, 1965), pp. 7–8.

be correct or erroneous in varying degrees. One thing, however, is sure: to the extent that his understanding and his attitude are true, they reflect a ray from "the true Light that enlightens every man" (Jn. 1:9).

In its Declaration on the Relation of the Church to Non-Christian Religion, Vatican II says:

> The Catholic Church rejects nothing that is true and holy in these religions. She regards with sincere reverence those ways of conduct and life, those precepts and teachings which, though differing in many aspects from the ones she holds and sets forth, nonetheless often reflect a ray of that Truth which enlightens all men (*NA* 2).

A non-Christian may indeed be interiorly enlightened by the Word of God who created him—the Word who sooner or later offers his light of grace to every man—and thus the Word of God is truly the criterion of this man's spirituality. Or, if he is not yet interiorly enlightened by grace but has merely adopted the religious attitudes of his fellowmen, to the extent that he is sincere and these attitudes do reflect a ray of the Word, he is open to receive the interior light.

All Religious Truth Leads to Christ

Though Vatican II teaches that what is true and holy in non-Christian religions can be a reflection from the Word of truth himself, in no way does it encourage syncretism or the notion that one religion or spirituality is as good as another.

All that is "true and holy" in anyone's spirituality is somehow a reflection of the Truth who enlightens every man, because the creative Word and the redemptive Word are one same Person, and all revelation given by God—whether in his action of creating and providentially bringing his creation to its perfection, or in his redeeming action in his Chosen People in Christ and in his Church—is but a ray from the Incarnate Word in whom all revelation is completed. Any partial ray must lead to the full brightness of "the Sun of Justice" (Mal. 3:20, c).

We do not have the whole truth until all the partial revelations of God are seen in their unity and fullness in Christ. Thus Christ, the living Gospel, the authentic man, is the norm of all spirituality. All authentic spirituality is at least implicitly Christological; "No one comes to the Father but by me" (Jn. 14:7).

The statement of Vatican II that the truth and holiness in non-Christian religions reflects a ray of truth from the Word of God is implicitly an insistence that all men are called to the Incarnate Word to find in him the fullness of truth, the fullness of God's self-revelation and self-communication. Therefore, in the next sentence the Council says explicitly: "Indeed, the Church proclaims and must ever proclaim Christ, 'the way, the truth and the life' (Jn. 14:6), in whom men find the fullness of religious life, and in whom God has reconciled all things to himself (2 Cor. 5:18–19)" (*NA* 2).

All True Spirituality Is Paschal

In *Gaudium et Spes,* Vatican II teaches explicitly that all spirituality is one, and that all mankind can somehow participate in the paschal mystery of Christ. After showing how Christ is the revelation of authentic man and how only in the paschal mystery can man be restored to the image and likeness of God, the Council declares:

All this holds true not only for Christians, but for all men of good will in whose hearts grace works in an unseen way. For since Christ died for all men, and since the ultimate vocation of man is in fact one and divine, we must believe that the Holy Spirit in a manner known only to God offers to every man the possibility of being associated with this paschal mystery. Such is the mystery of man. . . . (*GS* 22).

In other words, all men are called to find the completion and fullness of their spirituality in Christian spirituality—in Christ and his paschal mystery, in Christ and his Church, the living Gospel. The very structure of man as created by God cries out for Christ and for God's gift of himself to man in the mystery of Christ.

A man's spirituality may be an existential attitude resulting from his understanding of God as revealed in creation. However, if this spirituality is to be fruitful in true communion with God, "the Holy Spirit in a manner known only to God" (*GS* 22) has to be at work in this man. Indeed, only through the light of the Holy Spirit—the light of the Word who enlightens every man—can man interpret the signs of God in creation as an invitation to man to find communion with God.[17] Thus all viable, effective spirituality really begins with God working in man through the inner grace of the Holy Spirit.

[17] God cannot be met in sheer nature. The revelation of God in creation of itself is not enough to bring man to an effective encounter with God. On this, see Alszeghy and Flick, "A Personalistic View of Original Sin," *Theology Digest*, 15 (1967), pp. 193f. See also A. Hulsbosch as quoted above.

Latent or Anonymous Christians

Any non-Christian who is enlightened by the word that enlightens every man is implicitly a Christian, is under the
New Law, and belongs to the Church in some way (cf. *LG*
16; *GS* 22); that is, on condition that his enlightenment is a
true interior word of grace, an interior mission of the divine
Person of the Word, an "illumination which breaks forth
into the affection of love."[18] For a mission of the Word is
always inseparable from a mission of the Holy Spirit of love.

St. Thomas teaches that the men of the Old Testament
who had charity and the grace of the Holy Spirit really be-
longed to the new and eternal covenant, and therefore be-
longed to the Church, the Mystical Body of Christ.[19] The
same would be true of any member of the human race, pagan
or otherwise, who had received the grace of the Holy Spirit
and charity.[20] These truths are clearly affirmed by Vatican II
(*LG* 16; *GS* 22).

One Spirituality for All

We see, then, why there is but one authentic spirituality for
all mankind, the Gospel spirituality. Christian spirituality
explicitly accepts as its criterion Christ and his Gospel, other
spiritualities implicitly accept him and his Gospel to the
extent that they reflect a ray from the Word, who calls all
men to the one same hope. "The ultimate vocation of man

[18] St. Thomas Aquinas, *Summa Theologica*, I, Q. 43, a. 5, ad 2.
[19] *Ibid.*, Ia–IIae, Q. 107, a. 1, ad 2, and III, Q. 8, a. 3, ad 3.
[20] Karl Rahner explains how this could be true even of an atheist.
"Atheism and Implicit Christianity," *Theology Digest*, Sesquicenten-
nial Issue (February, 1968), pp. 43–56. See also "Rahner's 'Anonymous'
Christian," *Theology Digest*, 13 (Autumn, 1965), pp. 163–171.

is in fact one and divine" (*GS* 22). Created to be a son of God, man can be a son only in the Son.

Authentic human spirituality is one not only by reason of man's ultimate vocation but also by reason of his creation. "In the image of God he created them" (Gen. 1:27). The word translated as "created" really means "begot as sons." The passage could be rendered, "In the image of God he begot them as sons."[21]

One Spirituality Incarnate in Differing "Spiritualities"

There is, then, only one authentic spirituality for all mankind. Christ the Word is the "author and finisher" of spirituality, the beginning and the goal (Heb. 12:2). He is "the Alpha and Omega" (*GS* 45; Apoc: 1:8), containing in himself the whole alphabet of meaning, all the truth that can be expressed in thought, word and action, and is therefore the answer to every question that can be asked. He is presented by Vatican II (*GS* 41) as an answer to all burning questions of our times: What is man? What is God? What is the end of all things?

[21] We are indebted to Father Philip Roets, C.SS.R., for this interpretation, whose explanation is as follows: The Hebrew word, bārā', is a "Lamedh-Aleph" verb, a type of verb current at the end of the Old Testament times, and is traceable to the Aramaic influence of the second and first centuries B.C. The first syllable, bār, is the Aramaic word for son. The use of this verb only in verses 1:1–2, 27, and 2:3 of Genesis is highly indicative of its theological importance. See Francis Brown, S. R. Driver, and C. A. Briggs, *A Hebrew and English Lexicon of the Old Testament* (Boston: Houghton Mifflin, 1907), p. 135, cols. 1–2; also Francis Zorell, S.J., *Lexicon Hebraicum et Aramaicum Veteris Testamenti* (1951), p. 125, col. 2.

Though there is but one authentic spirituality, that of the paschal mystery, there are a multitude of authentic "spiritualities" in the sense that there are numerous valid styles of living the one true spirituality. For if the Gospel has to become "incarnate" in the differing human cultures of various times and places, then there are many spiritualities, many ways of living the one Gospel, the one mystery of Christ.

Each One's Spirituality Unique

In fact, there are as many kinds of spirituality as there are spiritual men. For each man's spirituality is uniquely his own. Spirituality, we have seen, is not something abstract from life; it is life itself organized in relationship with God, it is a man's practical, existential attitude toward God; and so each man's spirituality is uniquely personal.

Moreover, a spirituality can be effective only when it is a response to a personal vocation and interior grace from God, a unique personal call—"He calls his own sheep by name" (Jn. 10:3). One can come into effective communion with God only by the call of his grace and through his response in faith, and always and only in the paschal mystery of Christ (GS 22).

With these considerations in mind, we are ready for a fuller definition of spirituality than Hans Urs von Balthasar's general one presented earlier in this chapter. His definition was intended to cover all spirituality, whether true or false. But since all authentic spirituality is implicitly Christian and must become ever more explicitly so, let us consider a definition of explicitly Christian spirituality.

Definition of Christian Spirituality

In his definition, Father Albert-Marie Besnard, O.P., defines spirituality very concretely, as something very personal, unique to each individual, but also as within the universal paschal mystery. For the mystery of Christ, the universal norm of all authentic spirituality, contains certain invariables which have to be embodied in each man's life in a uniquely personal way.

Spirituality is the structuring of an adult personality in faith, according to one's proper genius, vocation and charismatic gifts on the one hand, and according to the laws of the universal Christian mystery on the other.[22]

In a later volume, we shall consider in more detail how each one's unique vocation from God is the criterion of his personal spirituality. Let us consider now, however, the universal Christian mystery as the criterion of everyone's spirituality—the invariables of authentic spirituality of every place and era, the elements which should be embodied in every culture and in the personal spirituality of each individual. These invariables are revealed in Christ, the Authentic Man.

[22] "Tendencies of Contemporary Spirituality," *Spirituality in the Church and World,* Concilium IX (New York: The Paulist Press, 1965), p. 26.

Part Three

AUTHENTIC MAN: THE INVARIABLES OF CHRISTIAN SPIRITUALITY

We have noted the necessity, especially for our times, of presenting Christian spirituality in anthropological and incarnational terms. For modern man is intensely man-centered and concerned about human fulfillment. Authentic spirituality, of course, guarantees that man will be his true self, both as an individual and in community.

In *Gaudium et Spes,* Vatican II presented a Christian anthropology as seen in Christ, the authentic man. Each chapter of the first part of the document, beginning always with universally accepted truths about man, ends with a section showing how these truths are eminently verified in Christ (*GS* 10, 22, 32, 38–39, 45).

In this third part of our book, we shall present the invariables of Christian spirituality in the light of Christ, authentic man, as presented by Vatican II.

11

AUTHENTIC MAN:
SON OF THE FATHER

The contemporary world is intensely interested in man. Man is the center of everything, he is the lord of the world who through science and technology has at last, it seems, achieved dominion over the universe.

This keen interest in man in our times has been accompanied, fortunately, by the rediscovery of Jesus as man. This rediscovery has been a blessing, for it enables us to represent Christian spirituality as the authentic humanism, the true answer to the humanistic quest of our times.

Since spirituality is man's participation in the life of God, authentic spirituality requires accurate concepts both of man and of God. It is in Christ that we find the revelation of both concepts:

Only in the mystery of the Incarnate Word does the mystery

of man take on light. . . . He who is "the image of the invisible
God" is himself the perfect man. . . .

By the revelation of the mystery of the Father and his love,
Christ fully reveals man to himself, and makes his supreme calling clear (*GS* 22).

The rediscovery of Jesus as man is truly the rediscovery of
every man as son of God: son of the Father's love, created in
love through the Word, restored in redemptive love in the
Incarnate Word, called to live in filial love as a son in the
Son, in his communion with the Father in the Holy Spirit.

The Rediscovery of Jesus as Man

What do we mean by saying that Jesus has been rediscovered
as Man?

In recent centuries, there has been a tendency to so con-
centrate upon the divinity of Christ and his sublime perfections that we did not always realize clearly enough the full
reality of his humanity. We did not fully contemplate and
savor the truth that Jesus, Son of the living God, was truly
"like us in all things except sin" (cf. Heb. 4:15). We did not
appreciate enough the truth presented by Hebrews that Jesus
became perfect, he developed as man, he grew in a human
way toward perfection; and this precisely through sufferings
and obedience (Heb. 2:10; 5:7–10).

Only in filial obedience did he come to his full lordship
over the world, thereby showing mankind that this alone is
the way to the dominion which modern man is seeking so
ardently. Because he was "obedient unto death" God has
highly exalted him, so that "every tongue should confess that
Jesus Christ is *Lord*" (Phil. 2:8, 11).

The rediscovery of Jesus as fully man does not in the least

derogate from his divinity, his dignity as God's eternal Son. "Son though he was," says Hebrews, "he learned obedience through what he suffered" (Heb. 5:8), coming to his perfection as man in a human way; that is, by personal choice, in willing obedience, accepting his sufferings in filial love and reverence for the Father.

Authentic Man:
Son of God in Filial Obedience

Thus Jesus has been rediscovered as the prototype of man, the authentic man: man created in the image and likeness of God and given dominion over the world, man who is son of God and lord of the world through loving obedience, man on a journey through sufferings to the Father in heaven who loves him, and to whom he responds in love.

For the filial reverence of Jesus of which Hebrews speaks (Heb. 5:7), is a son's response to the Father's love. Jesus fully manifested that he is son of God precisely by his unwavering reverence for the Father even in the face of death.

He was certainly conscious of his Father's love for him: "As the Father has loved me, so have I loved you . . ." (Jn. 15:9). "For this reason the Father loves me, because I lay down my life that I may take it again" (Jn. 10:17). "He who sent me is with me; he has not left me alone, for I always do what is pleasing to him" (Jn. 8:29).

To this love, Jesus responded by going forth to his sufferings and death: "I do as the Father has commanded me, so that the world may know that I love the Father. Rise, let us go hence" (Jn. 14:31).

All these passages clearly show the mutual personal relationships of Jesus and the Father in knowledge and in love.

His consciousness of the Father's love for him brings forth his human response of love in filial obedience.

Jesus thus reveals that authentic man is he who shows himself a true son of God through loving obedience.

Only through his obedience perfected in suffering, only by becoming humanly perfect through his personal choice of the Father in filial love, did Jesus become the cause of divine sonship for the rest of us: "Though he was a son, he learned obedience through what he suffered; and being made perfect, he became the source of eternal salvation to all who obey him" (Heb. 5:8–9).

This salvation, achieved through obedience in the obedience of Jesus consists in becoming sons in the Son:

> For it was fitting that he, for whom and by whom all things exist, in bringing many sons to glory, should make the pioneer of their salvation perfect through suffering. For he who sanctifies and those who are sanctified have all one origin. That is why he is not ashamed to call them brethren (Heb. 2:10–12).

In the Son, there are many sons, brothers of Jesus the Son. In the obedience of Christ, man is restored to authentic humanity—restored in the image and likeness of God and to the dominion over the world which God had given him in the beginning.

The rediscovery of Jesus as fully man, then, does not derogate from his dignity as Son of God, but does greatly enhance man's dignity as son of God in the Son.

Man: Image of God

Thus it is clear that the mystery of man and the mystery of Christ are but one mystery. "For Adam, the first man, was a figure of him who was to come, namely, Christ the Lord" (*GS* 22). Adam, the foreshadowing, gives place to Christ the Lord, the full reality.

Genesis teaches that man is the image of God precisely by reason of his lordship over the world which God has entrusted to him. Jesus, however, exalted to Lordship over the universe only because of his obedient service in sufferings, reveals that filial obedience to the Father is the only possible way to rightful dominion over the world; only a son rightfully rules in the Father's house. Man has his true dominion over God's creation because he is a son of God, image of the Father, and as son does always the things that please the Father.

Thus authentic man, son of the Father, having dominion in the Father's house, is revealed to us in the Paschal Mystery of Jesus. "Now the slave's place in the house is not assured, but the son's place is assured" (Jn. 8:35, j). "Moses was faithful in the house of God, but as a servant . . . Christ was faithful as a son, and as the master in the house" (Heb. 3:5–6, j).

Authentic Man:
Participant in the Paschal Mystery

It is as Servant-King, then, that Jesus reveals man to man; that is, as the suffering Servant of Yahweh who became Lord of all only because as Son of God he was obedient to the Father, even unto death on a cross.

But not only is Jesus the prototype of the true man; he alone is the source of the true humanity: "Being made perfect, he became the source of eternal salvation to all who obey him" (Heb. 5:9). Having passed through death to the

Father, and been exalted as Lord of the world, he has received for us the Holy Spirit, the fruit of his Paschal Mystery,
the Spirit in whom we cry, "Abba," the Spirit in whom
alone we can be sons of the Father and therefore authentic
men. He who participates in the Paschal Mystery, he who
receives from the Lord the gift of the Holy Spirit, and in the
Holy Spirit enters into the filial obedience of Jesus, is an
authentic man.

This is the meaning of the teaching of Vatican II that the
risen man is the authentic man: "For Adam, the first man,
was a figure of him who was to come, namely, Christ the
Lord" (*GS* 22). It is as Lord that Christ is the true man. In
the Scriptures, "Lord" is his title precisely as the man risen
from the dead and exalted to the presence of God because
of his obedience. Thus only he who participates in the Lord's
Paschal Mystery, in his death and resurrection, is authentic
man.

The Authentic Humanism

The paragraph in which Vatican II declares that Jesus reveals man to man (*GS* 22) was originally entitled "Christ,
the Perfect Man." But this was changed to read "Christ, the
New Man," to signify all the more strikingly that Christ
is no mere evolutionary unfolding and development in
human history but is the Incarnate Word's sudden, transcendent "breaking into" the universe to transfigure it.

For the first man was of the earth, earthly; the second
Adam is from heaven, heavenly (1 Cor. 15:47). Every man
is called to be a heavenly man in Christ, an adopted son of
the eternal Father, in the Holy Spirit. *This* is the authentic
man as intended by the Creator in making man to his own

image and likeness. "Christ, 'the image of the invisible God'
. . . restores to the sons of Adam the divine likeness which
had been disfigured from the first sin onward" (*GS* 22).
Image of God by his very nature, man becomes the full likeness of God only when he is transfigured by the supernatural
gift of divine sonship in the risen Christ.

It is precisely here, in this divine gift of life from above,
that the difference between Christianity and mere humanism
is manifest. Man is no mere lord of the world; he is son of
God called to live in communion with the heavenly Father,
"chosen to live through love in his presence" (Eph. 1:4, j).
Moreover, man is no mere evolutionary unfolding and development in history; authentic man is "from heaven, heavenly." Not only is the Incarnation of the Word a "breaking
into" the universe from above, but so is the begetting of any
man "from above" (Jn. 3:3, a) when he is born again in the
risen Christ of water and the Holy Spirit.

12

AUTHENTIC MAN: SERVANT OF HIS BROTHERS

When *Gaudium et Spes* presents Jesus in his Paschal Mystery as the authentic man—Jesus, the Servant-Lord who came to his dominion only through obedience—it is in response to specific needs of our times.

Contemporary man, we said, is avid to rule the world, to master it by his science and technology; and, in fact, because of his increasing dominion over it, it sometimes seems to him that he no longer needs a God—"God is dead!"

And yet, in spite of his growing mastery over nature, man is experiencing the paradox of ever increasing misery among his fellowmen, along with the danger that the very technology which makes him lord of the world will be his destruction. The very hope which man places in his dominion over the world is thus accompanied by fear and anxiety.

The answer to the distress and anxiety of our contemporaries is Jesus, the true man, who himself journeyed to the Father through the distress and anguish of sufferings, sufferings by which he rendered a service to his fellowmen. The absurdity of life, experienced so intensely by modern man, finds its answer in the absurdity of the Cross, the foolishness which is the wisdom of God (1 Cor. 1).

Service, the Purpose of Dominion

As Servant of Yahweh who comes to his lordship only in suffering and in service, Jesus shows not merely the true way to dominion over the world but also the true purpose of this dominion. The increasing misery of mankind at the very time when man seems to be winning dominion over the world through technology reveals that mankind has not yet achieved the authentic dominion which is found only in the obedient sonship of Christ; he has not exercised his dominion for the right purpose, the service of his fellowmen.

For dominion without true brotherhood among men is dominion without divine sonship. Dominion without brotherhood turns into the tyranny of the few, whether political or economic, and the misery of the many.

Man's dominion over the world is authentic, fruitful and complete, only when it is exercised in obedience to the God-given purposes revealed in Christ, the Servant-Lord, whose divine humanism is expressed in his declaration: "The Son of Man has come not to be served but to serve, and give his life as a ransom for many" (Mk. 10:45). The Father wills that man be master over nature only that he might use this dominion in the service of his brothers.

Son and Servant

Christ, who reveals all this to us in his own person, stands out as the true image of God in a twofold personal relationship: Son of the Father and Servant of his brethren. Son and Servant—these two realities in Christ, the authentic man, are the fulfillment of the two realities expressed about man in the Book of Genesis: he is the image of God and is given dominion over the world. Christ is the image of God precisely because he is Son of the Father, for a son is his father's likeness; and he has dominion through his filial obedience in the service of his brethren. Man is fully image of God only when he is son of the Father in the eternal Son; and he exercises rightful dominion over the earth only when he develops the earth in the service of his brothers, using the goods the Father has entrusted to him for their benefit.

Spirituality of Work

These are the truths emphasized and lived in the Servant Spirituality which emerged in Vatican II. Against this background, *Gaudium et Spes* presents its beautiful spirituality of work and social cooperation:

When man develops the earth by the work of his hands or with the aid of technology, in order that it might bear fruit and become a dwelling worthy of the whole human family, and when he consciously takes part in the life of social groups, he carries out the design of God manifested at the beginning of time, that he should subdue the earth, perfect creation, and develop himself. At the same time, he obeys the commandment of Christ that he place himself at the service of his brethren (*GS* 57).

Moreover, the Council declares, a man's daily work is his basic service to his fellowmen, and therefore should be one of his most fundamental expressions of Christian love (*GS* 67).

Christ, the Servant-Lord, thus reveals the true meaning and purpose of man's dominion over the world. He is master of nature, not that his dominion might degenerate into a tyranny over his fellowmen nor that he might egoistically hoard the fruits of the earth and of his industry for himself alone. God has given him dominion only for the sake of service. He is not enslaved by his possessions, imprisoned by his greed for them; he is the free master of whatever he owns, as a son in his father's house freely dispensing the gifts of the father in love for his brothers.

The Divine Humanism:
Universal Fraternal Love

This servant spirituality crowns and completes, Christianizes, the humanism of our times.

For in response to the increasing misery of the masses in modern times, a new humanism is arising "one in which man is defined first of all by his responsibility to his brothers and to history" (*GS* 55).

Jesus is the model who shows this humanism in its perfection, and the Holy Spirit whom he gives us as the fruit of his own paschal obedience gives mankind the power to fulfill its responsibilities.

For only in the Holy Spirit can man be "son in the Son" (*GS* 22) and "capable of discharging the new law of love" (*GS* 22). In keeping this law he builds the universal brotherhood in which alone man can be authentic man. "As the

firstborn of many brethren and by the giving of his Spirit,
Jesus founded after his death and resurrection a new brotherly community composed of all those who receive him in
faith and love" (*GS* 32). This community in the resurrection
is achieved only in the laying down of one's life for the
brethren (*ibid.*).

For the cry "Abba, Father," inspired by the Holy Spirit,
does not have its full truth until the child of God can pronounce it in a universal brotherhood.

Universal Spirituality and Conscience

Vatican II speaks much of this "universal brotherhood" (*GS*
38). Christian spirituality has always emphasized love of
neighbor, accepting him as brother. Contemporary spirituality puts very special emphasis upon the universality of this
brotherhood. In these times when man is consciously striving
for one world, and speedy communications are impelling
him toward it, a Christian can no longer restrict his practice
of effective love to the small group within which he lives—
his family, his clan, his local community, his religious community. Still less can there be anything individualistic about
his spirituality. The spirituality of today must carefully cultivate a universal conscience, a conscience accepting its
responsibility for the unity of all mankind.

Vatican II returns frequently to this truth; for example:

Since the Church is in Christ like a sacrament or as a sign and
instrument both of a very closely knit union with God and of
the unity of the whole human race, it desires now to unfold more
fully to the faithful of the Church and to the whole world its
own inner nature and universal mission. . . . The present-day

conditions of the world add greater urgency to this work of the
Church so that all men, joined more closely today by various
social, technical and cultural ties, might also attain fuller unity
in Christ (*LG* 1).

Or again: "profound and rapid changes make it more necessary that no one, ignoring the trend of events or drugged
by laziness, content himself with a merely individualistic
morality" (*GS* 30). Each person fulfills the obligations of
justice and love only by accepting his responsibilities in caring for the needs of society and in bettering the conditions
of human life. "As citizens of two cities" Christians may not
"shirk their earthly responsibilities" (*GS* 43).

There can be no authentic spirituality, then, without this
universal conscience, this responsibility for the universal
brotherhood. Nor is this a hopeless task. In the Risen Christ,
the authentic man, the hopelessness and anxiety of our times
can and must be replaced by a firm hope and persevering
effort for unity and peace among men. Because God's Word
has "entered the world's history as a perfect man, taking that
history up into himself and bringing it under his headship
. . . the effort to establish a universal brotherhood is not a
hopeless one. . . . Appointed Lord by his resurrection and
given all power in heaven and on earth, Christ is now at
work in the hearts of men through the energy of his Spirit
. . ." (*GS* 38).

13

AUTHENTIC MAN: IN COMMUNION WITH THE FATHER

The authentic man is son and servant. As son—image of God—he rejoices in the contemplation of the Father. As servant—with dominion over the Father's household—he is ever eager to be of help to his brothers.

Man's Integral Vocation

In the chapter in *Gaudium et Spes* entitled "The Dignity of the Human Person," Vatican II recalls from Genesis that "man was created 'to the image of God' " and was given dominion over all earthly creatures (*GS* 12). It then consistently shows, throughout the entire Constitution, that both these elements belong to the integral vocation of man. Neither may be neglected at the expense of the other.

First, as image of God, "capable of knowing and loving

124

his Creator" (*GS* 12), man was made for friendship with God, for loving communion with him. And secondly, by reason of his dominion over other creatures, he was given a task in the world.

The true meaning of both is found in Jesus, Son and Servant.

A son is his father's likeness. Christ is image of the invisible God because he is the Father's Son. As Son of the Father, he lives ever with the Father in a perfect communion of love in the Holy Spirit.

As servant, sent on a mission by the Father, he renders the service which is essentially the bringing of all mankind into his own sonship and filial communion with the Father. "Jesus, knowing that the Father had given all things into his hands, and that he had come from God and was going to God," said, "I go to prepare a place for you. And when I go and prepare a place for you, I will come again and will take you to myself, that where I am you may be also" (Jn. 13:3; 14:2–3).

The Vertical Dimension

Man is the image of God to the extent that he, too, as "son in the Son" (*GS* 22), enters into filial communion with the Father in the Holy Spirit of the Son:

The basic source of human dignity lies in man's call to communion with God. From his very origin man is already invited to converse with God. For he exists only because he is created by God's love and is constantly preserved by it. Nor does he live fully according to truth unless he freely acknowledges that love and commits himself to his Creator (*GS* 19).

Vatican II thus reasserts the vertical dimension of man—his direct personal relationship with God his Father.

Jean Mouroux beautifully expresses these truths in his commentary on *Gaudium et Spes* 22:

Man is revealed to man by that which is most intimate and profound in the mystery of Christ: his personal relationship with his Father, his sonship. The Council thus puts itself in opposition to every sort of anthropocentrism. The secret of man is in God. The secret is that man is loved by the Father and saved by him in Christ and in the Spirit. It is only when man has discovered that mystery that he can be fully revealed to himself as a son of God, redeemed by Christ, destined to receive the *agape* of the Father, and to live for all men his brothers.

It is therefore by participation in the mystery of trinitarian relationships that men are fulfilled and discover that they are "sons in the Son" (*GS* 22). . . .

The true revelation of man is the revelation of the true God; and the two are bound together in Jesus Christ, God made man.[23]

Thus in Jesus are revealed the answers to the great contemporary questions (which indeed are man's perennial questions, built into his very nature as quest): What is man? What is God?[24] Man is truly man only when he is son of

---

[23] "Sur la dignité de la personne humaine," *L'Eglise dans le monde de ce temps*, II, *Unam Sanctam* 65b (Paris: Editions du Cerf, 1967), p. 249.

[24] Recall the words of Jesus to St. Catherine of Siena: "Daughter, do you know who you are and who I am? If you know these two things you will be happy. I am he who is, you are she who is not." Building upon this basic lesson, Jesus leads Catherine to understand eventually, that though she is naught by herself, through union with him in faith and love, she becomes "Another Himself."

God, sharing in the life of the Holy Trinity, participating
in the eternal Son's filial relationship with the Father in the
Spirit who is love. Only in the Holy Spirit can we live in
filial relationship with the Father, and thus be the very
image of God.

Image as Presence of God

Image, in the Scriptures, signifies not merely a representa-
tion, but a kind of true presence of the one represented. Man
is a presence of God to his fellowmen when God abides in
him and he in God—when God enters him, pouring forth
his love into him in the gift of the Holy Spirit of love. Thus
deeply involved in the intimate personal relationships of the
Holy Trinity, man reveals the presence of the Trinity (*GS*
21).[25] Son of the Father in the Spirit, he shows forth the
Father's love in brotherly love of his fellowmen.

Here we have perhaps the most profound reason for speaking of incarnational spirituality. Man's personal relationships
in Christ with the Father and with his brothers is a kind of
incarnation of the divine life in mankind. We shall return to
this idea when we speak of the Christian fellowship.

The Rediscovery of Jesus as God

The rediscovery of Jesus as man is truly the rediscovery of
Jesus as God. "He is man not in spite of the fact that he is
God, but because he is God. . . . Consecrated interiorly, trans-

---

[25] See above, Chapter 8, under the subheading "Witness to the Living
Gospel."

figured in the glory of Tabor, he remains human, because man is created in the image of God."[26]

This man who is God reveals what God intended every man should be: a participant in God's own life, a son in communion with the Father in heaven. "In truth, it is only in the mystery of the Word Incarnate that the mystery of man is truly clarified" (*GS* 22).

The Horizontal Dimension: Building Universal Brotherhood

Christ as Son, in direct personal relationship with God his Father, reveals, we said, the indispensable vertical dimension of authentic man. But Christ is not only Son of the Father, he is also servant of his brothers. Christ's mission of service reveals, therefore, the meaning and purpose of man's dominion over the earth, the horizontal dimension of his life.

Our Lord's greatest service to his brothers is his revelation of the Father, his bringing them to the Father in this revelation. His mission to bring his fellowmen into communion with the Father is the pattern of every man's mission in the world.

It is every man's mission to serve his fellowmen, first, by bearing witness to the call of all to divine sonship and communion with God. But only by living in that communion can one bear witness to it. Only he who is in that communion is image of the invisible God, in the twofold sense of likeness and presence of the God who is shown forth.

Secondly, every man has the mission to serve his brothers

---

[26] Charles Moeller, "Perspectives oecumeniques postconciliares," *L'Eglise dans le monde de ce temps*, III, *Unam Sanctam* 65c (Paris: Editions du Cerf, 1967), p. 180.

by cooperating with them in love's task of making the world more human, a fitting dwelling place for the sons of God, a world more open to God. In this rightly ordered earthly home, God's children can grow to maturity in preparation for their being taken home to the Father.

Thus man's mission on earth is to build the universal brotherhood of the sons of the Father. The horizontal and vertical dimensions of Christian life are seen to be not at all in opposition with one another. The vertical dimension is communion with the Father, the horizontal dimension, the Christian task in the world, is to bring all mankind into this communion, to build a world more open to God, to bring all men into the joy of contemplating the Father. The Church, as "a people made one with the unity of the Father, the Son and the Holy Spirit" (*LG* 4), "is in Christ like a sacrament or sign and instrument of a very closely knit union with God, and of the unity of the whole human race" (*LG* 1).

14

THE INVARIABLES
OF CHRISTIAN SPIRITUALITY

We have spoken of the criteria of Christian spirituality—
the Word and the Spirit. The term "criterion," however,
could connote some sort of an exterior standard against
which we measure ourselves. Perhaps in speaking of the word
of God as a criterion we did give the impression that it is
merely an exterior norm. In speaking of the Spirit, however,
we showed that he is an interior witness and guide enlighten-
ing us from within, "interiorizing" the word of God in us,
writing it in our hearts (Jer. 31: 33; 2 Cor. 3:3), or, like an
unction, a penetrating oil, causing it to penetrate our understanding and to inspire our love (1 Jn. 2:21, 27).

But both Word and Spirit, as norms of spirituality, are
much more than interior light and guide; they are divine life
in us, they are an inner dynamic power (Eph. 1:19; 3:20).
When by the unction of the Holy Spirit the word of God

abides in our hearts, the very Person of the Word dwells in us and we in him, and we become sons of God in the Son. And we measure true to the Word of God, not as to some rule outside ourselves, but he, dwelling in us, fashions us from within into his own likeness—when we act according to his light and Spirit.

Let us therefore consider the essential interior qualities of Christian spirituality inasmuch as it is a sharing in God's own life, a participation in the Word and Holy Spirit, who have been sent to us in interior missions. We speak of these qualities as *invariables* because they are always present in authentic Christian spirituality, no matter how diversely the Christian life is embodied and expressed in differing personalities and cultures.

Become What You Are—and You Will Know Who You Are!

Spirituality, we said, is the recognition and acceptance of one's ontic relationships with God, and the structuring of one's action and personality accordingly. Nor is spirituality merely the structuring; it is the *life* which is so structured. Christian spirituality, then, as a participation in God's own life, is the recognition and acceptance, and the expression in our human action, of all those invariables, those essential qualities, which are planted in us in the very gift of the divine life in grace.

Growth in spirituality is thus a growth in self-awareness, an increasing recognition of what one *is* by the gift of God— and living true to it! It is a growing consciousness of ourself as a child of God and a sharer in the life of the Holy Trinity —and acting accordingly! Only thus can the Christian be authentic, only thus can he measure true to what he is. "Become what you are!" is a recurrent theme of St. Paul. That is, you are sons of God by grace; therefore grow up in this sonship by living as sons. "All who are led by the Spirit of God are sons of God" (Rom. 8:14); "If we live by the Spirit, let us also walk by the Spirit" (Gal. 5:25). If the Spirit is the principle of life in us, let us live that life—let us become ever more fully who we are by God's gift: "men of the Spirit" (1 Cor. 2:15).

Spirituality is thus a matter of being authentic—of living true to who we are by the grace of divine sonship.

Becoming Who We Are:
the Work of Prayer and Conscience

Becoming who we are is the work of a mature, rightly formed conscience, a conscience which is ever conscious of the invariables of Christian spirituality and is moved to embody them in every action of life. Only thus does one come to authentic personal fulfillment.

The invariables will be "alive" in our conscience, however, impelling us to the divine actions of the sons of God, only if we keep them in the forefront of our consciousness, and not merely buried somewhere deep in our memory. And this can be done only by frequent listening to the word of God and pondering it in our heart, and by fidelity in prayer, conversing frequently with the God with whom our whole life is to be an intimate relationship.

Frequent prayer is necessary, then, if our conscience is to be alive to God and to the requirements of divine sonship. Only a son who turns frequently to the Father in prayer will have the alert and ready conscience of a son. "He who sent me is with me; he has not left me alone, for I always do what is pleasing to him" (Jn. 8:29). The invariables, we shall see, consist in relationships with the three divine Persons; and when they are expressed in all of life, the whole life becomes a prayer, a living communion with Father, Son and Holy Spirit.

Christian Spirituality Is Always Paschal

There can be no communion with God except through participation in the death and resurrection of Jesus, the paschal mystery. "No one comes to the Father but by me" (Jn. 14:6). For all men are sinners, and can be children of God only by the grace of justification in Christ. "Scripture makes no exceptions when it says sin is master everywhere" (Gal. 3:22, j). The word of God is a judgment upon mankind, declaring that man has not measured true to God's will for him. The judgment upon Israel is true of all mankind.

" 'I will not serve,' you said" (Jer. 2:20). " 'I will not listen.' This has been your way from your youth, not to listen to my voice" (Jer. 22:21, c). "All nations," like Israel, follow "their own evil heart" (Jer. 3:17). "Man's every thought and all the inclinations of his heart were only evil" (Gen. 6:5, c).

By his disobedience, man had refused to live in the image and likeness of God, he had rejected divine sonship. "God has imprisoned all men in their own disobedience, only to show mercy to all mankind" (Rom. 11:32, j). "For as by one man's disobedience many were made sinners, so by one man's obedience many will be made righteous" (Rom. 5:19).

No man can come to God except in the obedience of Christ. We are baptized into this obedience, we enter into

Christ's paschal mystery, his obedient death and resurrection.
Or rather, we are "baptized into Christ Jesus" himself (Rom.
6:3), into the Person of the Incarnate Word. We enter into
his entire life, death and resurrection, so that this whole
mystery might be formed in us.

Authentic spirituality is therefore always Christological,
paschal, baptismal. "Become what you are" means: Live true
to what is signified and accomplished by your baptism. Baptism incorporated you into Christ in his paschal mystery so
that your whole life might be lived in union with him in the
likeness of this mystery. "We were buried therefore with
him by baptism into death . . . so that as Christ was raised
from the dead by the glory of the Father we too might walk
in newness of life. For if we have been united with him in a
death like his, we shall certainly be united with him in a
resurrection like his" (Rom. 6:4–5).

Christian Spirituality Is Always Ecclesial and Sacramental or Liturgical

Baptism is an ecclesial act, accomplished by the Church.
Incorporation into Christ the Head in baptism is incorporation into his Body, the Church, so that from that Body and
in that Body we may live the paschal mystery and be restored
to divine sonship.

As ecclesial, Christian spirituality is always a liturgical,
sacramental spirituality; especially, it is eucharistic. The
Church itself—and all its sacraments—is ever the sign and
instrument of Christ communicating his divine life and sonship to his members in the Church.

Thus, to live in the Church, the Body of Christ, is to live

in Christ the Head, to live the life of Christ, the Incarnate Word, whose divine sonship is, as it were, incarnate in his members. His total paschal mystery is incarnate in them, his dying as well as his resurrection. His dying is continued in his members so that his justification and glorification might be accomplished in them.

Christian Spirituality Is Always "in the Spirit"

Only in the Holy Spirit can we live the paschal mystery with Christ and thus become ever more truly the sons of God that we are by baptism. "If anyone does not have the Spirit of Christ he does not belong to Christ. But if Christ is in you . . . if the Spirit of him who raised Jesus is in you . . ." (Rom. 8:9–11, c). To have the Spirit is the same as to have Christ in you; he is the Spirit of Christ and of the Father who raised Jesus. To have the Spirit is to be a son of God in the Son, because we have "received a spirit of adoption as sons" (Rom. 8:15, c).

The Holy Spirit is the fruit of the paschal mystery of Jesus; to participate in this mystery is to live according to the Holy Spirit. For the paschal mystery is not merely the death and resurrection of Jesus, it is his sending of the Holy Spirit as the fruit of that mystery. Jesus goes to the Father in his death and glorification to receive from him for us the Spirit of adoption of sons. The mystery is completed in the sending of the Holy Spirit, it is completed in each of us to the extent that we "walk by the Spirit" (Gal. 5:25). The more one enters into the paschal mystery and lives it with Jesus, the more he is filled with the Holy Spirit.

Clearly, then, the only true devotion to the resurrection of

Jesus is the striving to be ever more filled with the Holy
Spirit who fashions us ever more fully in the sonship of
Christ.

Christian Spirituality Is Alway a
Dying with Christ

One can be filled with the Spirit, the risen life of Jesus, only
to the extent that one dies with Jesus. For the Spirit gives us
the resurrection, divine sonship in the risen Christ, only by
giving us the dying of Christ: "If by the Spirit you put to
death the deeds of the flesh, you will live" (Rom. 8:13, c).
The Spirit himself thus impels us to die with Christ in Christian mortification of "the flesh." Flesh, remember, means not
merely the body with its disorderly passions but man in his
unredeemed state. According to St. Paul, the redemption is
not totally completed merely by our incorporation into
Christ in baptism. Redemption is a continuing process in us
which goes on as the Spirit works in us, inspiring us to
mortify the flesh, the unredeemed area of self that continues
to coexist with "the spirit," the self as possessing the Spirit.

Here again it is a case of becoming what you are. You are
"spirit" once you have received the Spirit in baptism. But
live true to what you are by living according to the Spirit,
and by the grace of the Spirit putting to death the unredeemed self. Mortify the flesh by the Spirit and become ever
more a "man of the Spirit."

Here we have the basic reason for all Christian asceticism.
Its whole goal is to come ever more fully under the influence
of the Holy Spirit. We die with Christ so that we might live
with Christ; that is, so that we might live according to the
Holy Spirit. "For all who are led by the Spirit of God are

sons of God" (Rom. 8:14). Asceticism is thus an essential part of living the paschal mystery of Christ. We shall speak more fully of asceticism in a later volume.

Christian Spirituality Is Always Apostolic: a Sharing in Christ's Servant-Lordship

To the extent that his life truly is a participation in Christ's paschal mystery—in his dying and his coming to life in the Spirit—the Christian shares also in Christ's redeeming mission and apostolic power.

We have noted that the Christian conscience and spirituality must be universal, concerned about making the whole world more human, a place where men can truly be sons of God. His conscience will therefore impel him to do whatever he can, in keeping with his own situation and endowments, to carry on Christ's redeeming work, Christ's mission to transform "all flesh"—mankind still in process of being redeemed—into men of the Spirit, sons of God.

But each Christian's power in helping his fellowmen to become men of the Spirit is always in proportion to the extent that he himself is a man of the Spirit. On this point we must have no delusions. One cannot do the work of the Spirit unless he is possessed by the Spirit. Just as Jesus himself gives the Spirit only as the fruit of his paschal mystery—only because he has gone to the Father as the Suffering Servant in the loving obedience of his dying—so a Christian is a sacrament of Christ's redeeming work, a sign and instrument of his bestowing of the Spirit, only to the extent that the paschal mystery has been accomplished in him, only to the extent that he has died to self in humility and has surrendered himself into the possession of the Spirit.

He who would be an apostle must therefore become a suffering servant of Yahweh in Christ. According to St. Paul, hardships, labors, and sufferings are an essential mark of an authentic apostle (1 Cor. 4:9–13; 2 Cor. 6:4–10; 2 Cor. 11:23–12:10). And Paul is speaking not only of the original twelve, into whose company he himself has been taken. He means everyone who shares in any way in the redeeming mission of the Church. Participation in the paschal mystery involves the cross as well as the resurrection.

Therefore, twice he tells Timothy: "Take your share of sufferings" (2 Tim. 1:8 and 2:3). Your very grace of ordination, the laying on of hands, brings you a grace of fortitude for this purpose (*ibid.* 1:2). The laying on of hands in the sacrament of Confirmation does the same for every Christian. "Put up with your share of difficulties" (2 Tim. 2:3, j), he tells Timothy, and adds, "I have my own hardships to bear, even to being chained like a criminal—but they cannot chain up God's news" (2 Tim. 2:9, j).

Precisely because of Paul's chains, the good news is unchained. Paul's sufferings give power to the spread of the Gospel. "So I bear it all for the sake of those who are chosen" (2:10). This is a persistent teaching of St. Paul. "Death is at work in us," he tells the Corinthians, "but life in you" (2 Cor. 4:12). Because he is "always carrying in the body the death of Jesus" (*ibid.* 10), Christ's life is not only ever more manifest in his own person, but is also being communicated to others.

The same truth is expressed to the Colossians. "Now I rejoice in my sufferings for your sake, and in my flesh I complete what is lacking in Christ's afflictions for the sake of his body, that is, the Church, of which I have become a minister" (Col. 1:24–25). Paul does not mean that there is something deficient about Christ's sufferings, which are infinite in value. He means that they give their value to us only when the Church generously, lovingly suffers with Christ. The redemption is not completed in any generation until Christ's sufferings have been made present in that generation through the sufferings and labors of the Church, accepted in living faith and love. The sufferings of the Church—when they are lovingly, willingly accepted—are like a sacrament applying the benefits of Christ's sufferings in every time and place.

The apostle, the martyr, and indeed every Christian laboring and suffering for Christ, has the task of perfecting in his own person the Church's communion in the sufferings of her Saviour by loving openness and response to the suffering contained in the existential situation, the daily events of life, and thus making Christ's redemption effective in our times.

The Church is the fullness of Christ's risen life—his life in the Spirit and his power to give the Spirit—only to the extent that it is the fullness of his sufferings. And any member of the Church participates in this power to bring the Spirit to others only to the extent that he willingly participates in the humble and obedient dying of Christ, dying to self that he may be obedient to the Spirit.

"Here then is a saying that you can rely on: If we have died with him, then we shall live with him" (2 Tim. 2:11, j). Speaking in the context of his own physical sufferings in chains and the physical death which is facing him, Paul here means physical death in union with Christ, but as the perfecting of sacramental death. For elsewhere Paul has spoken of the sacramental dying and living with Christ in baptism (Rom. 6). Baptism, however, is only the beginning of our dying and rising with Christ. Each Christian's labors and hardships and sufferings and, finally, his physical death, are the completion of his sacramental death in baptism. "Baptized into his death" (Rom. 6:3), all our sufferings, ending in our physical death, are a dying with Christ—provided that in faithfulness to our baptismal grace we accept them in faith and love as a filling up of what is wanting to Christ's own sufferings, for our own progressive purification and redemption and for that of his Church.

Christian Spirituality:
Communion in the Holy Trinity

As a dynamic entering into Christ's sonship and paschal mystery, Christian life is an entering into the very life of the Holy Trinity.

The whole spiritual life has its origin in the Eternal Father and in the Son's eternal response to him in filial love in the Holy Spirit. All spirituality is a participation in this filial response of the Word, all spirituality is summed up in the one word of love in response to the love God has poured into our hearts—"Father!"

Christ's mission on earth is precisely to bring men into his own relationship to the Father as Son. "God sent his Son, born of a woman . . . so that we might receive the adoption as sons. And because you are sons, God has sent the Spirit of his Son into our hearts, crying 'Abba, Father!' " (Gal. 4:4–5). The visible mission of the Son is fulfilled in the invisible mission into our heart of the Spirit of the Son, who turns us toward the Father in the Son's own cry of love and joy.

Thus our adoption as sons is not some sort of mere extrinsic relationship to God in which we stand apart from the Holy Trinity in knowledge and love of them. It is an entering into the very relationships which the three divine Persons have among themselves, it is a participation in the very life of the Three. We are united to the Father in the same love in which Father and Son mutually love one another. Like the Word we can say: The Holy Spirit is not simply my love for the Father and the Father's love for me; he is our love, mutually proceeding from both of us. Poured into my heart from the Father's heart (Rom. 5:5), he simultaneously springs from my heart to the Father's heart in the cry "Abba!" which he inspires in me (Rom. 8:15).

Thus the Christian finds his God not "out there somewhere" above the heaven of heavens, but in his heart of hearts, closer to himself than he is to himself. The dogma of the Holy Trinity is not a meaningless intellectual abstraction or a figment of the imagination. Christians in every century have deeply experienced their lives as a participation in the very life of the Holy Trinity. They have testified to the verification in their own lives of our Lord's promise, "We will come and make our home with him" (Jn. 14:23).

Christian Spirituality: Fraternal Communion

These sons in the Son, participating in Christ's filial Spirit, are the Church, the People of God. Sharing in the very life of the Trinity, they are "a People made one in the unity of the Father and of the Son and of the Holy Spirit" (*LG* 4).

Our presence with the Father in the Word and Spirit, and his presence with us, our participation in the personal relationships of the Holy Trinity, is called, in the Scriptures, *koinonia,* translated either as "fellowship" or as "communion."

We prefer the translation "communion," because for most people the word "fellowship" has too superficial a connotation; it suggests mere comradeship, friendliness, companionship, or the "good fellowship" of drinking parties. It does not sufficiently connote profound communion in love and life.

Moreover, even the scriptural use of the word is being interpreted by many in an exclusively humanistic and secularistic way, emptying it of all sacred and Trinitarian content. For example, a professor of Scripture in a Midwest seminary, taking exception to one of this author's writings on *koinonia*,[27] wrote in a letter: "Liturgy, for me, is having a sandwich and a glass of beer in a tavern with one of my fellowmen."

"Good fellowship" of this kind can indeed be one of the expressions of our interior communion with God in his Son, but unfortunately present-day secularization often tends to reduce the fellowship to mere human interchange. However, as Father Yves Congar writes: "Christianity is not simply 'togetherness'. . . . *Koinonia* in the sense in which the word is used in the New Testament . . . is not that of a simple associative bond but that of a vertical participation in the same good, Christ, creating a unity or communion among the members."[28]

As a participation in Christ's sonship, *koinonia* is essentially communion in the Holy Trinity. This is evident from the fact that in the Scriptures the Holy Spirit—as given to us by the love of the Father in the grace of Jesus Christ—is himself practically called "the communion," since he is the bond of communion: "The grace of our Lord Jesus Christ

[27] "Christian Fellowship in the Epistle to the Philippians," *The Bible Today,* April, 1964.

[28] "Institutionalized Religion," in T. Patrick Burke, ed., *The Word in History* (New York: Sheed and Ward, 1966), pp. 134–135.

and the love of God and the fellowship (*koinonia*) of the Holy Spirit be with you all" (2 Cor. 13:13).

One cannot possess the Holy Spirit without being, in him, in communion with the Father and the Son: "Our fellowship is with the Father and with his Son Jesus Christ" (1 Jn. 1:3).

We receive this communion in the Trinity only in communion with the Apostles and the Church, for only through faith in the Gospel proclaimed by the Apostles do we receive the communion of the Spirit: "That which we have seen and heard we announce to you also, in order that you may have communion with us; yes, and our communion is with the Father and with his Son Jesus Christ" (1 Jn. 1:3, s).

Acts, too, describes the fellowship as following upon the gift of the Holy Spirit to those who believe (Acts 2:38–39) and who remain steadfast in the teaching of the Apostles (Acts 2:42). They who are in the Trinitarian communion in the Spirit are also in communion with one another: "And they devoted themselves to the apostles' teaching and fellowship, to the breaking of bread and the prayers" (Acts 2:42). The fellowship as spoken of in this text is really an expression, in ordinary daily life, of the interior communion with God and with one another. The communion in the Spirit is incarnate in the community action of love, it is embodied in effective works of mutual help.

The Eucharistic Koinonia (*1 Cor. 10:16–17*)

The eucharistic communion—"the breaking of the bread" (Acts 2:42)—is a sacrament of our communion with one another in the communion with the Trinity. It brings us more deeply into the Holy Trinity and therefore closer to one another.

For the Eucharist is communion in the paschal mystery, in which Jesus is manifest as true Son of the Father by his loving obedience in the Holy Spirit, and in which he takes us ever more intimately into this obedient sonship and communion with the Father. This he does by pouring the fruit of that paschal mystery, his Holy Spirit, more fully into our hearts.

Deeper communion with the Father in the paschal mystery is simultaneously deeper communion with all the children of the Father in the Holy Spirit. "The cup of blessing which we bless, is it not a communion (*koinonia*) in the blood of Christ? The bread which we break, is it not a communion in the body of Christ? Because there is one bread, we who are many are one body, for we all partake of the one bread" (1 Cor. 10:16–17). As one body of Christ, one mystical person with him in the paschal mystery, we are sons in the Son, brothers of one another.

The Prayers

The fourth essential element in the Christian community, "the prayers" (Acts 2:42)—liturgical prayer—are sung "with one accord," expressing the communion in praise and in thanksgiving that God has gathered his family together as one in the Holy Spirit.

Koinonia *Incarnate in Christian Righteousness*

Indeed the fellowship as expressed in effective love in daily life is not merely a haphazard conglomeration of works of

love performed as the need arises. The communion is incarnate in the very structuring of the Christian community
as the Body of Christ in "righteousness and peace and joy in
the Holy Spirit" (Rom. 14:17). Righteousness, we have seen,
is the rightness of all relationships between man and God
and between man and fellowman, a rightness which is the
gift of Christ in the Holy Spirit. In the thinking of St. Paul,
the love of neighbor which is the fulfillment of the law
consists in this righteousness, which is the sum total of all
the moral virtues as the expression of faith, hope and love.

To thus express our communion with God in effective
communion with our fellowmen is to deepen our communion with God. The community works of love and righteousness are like a sacrament in which we can receive a new mission of the Holy Spirit. For the unseen God is seen in our
neighbor (1 Jn. 4:20), who is thus a sacrament or sign of
God, and the very effort to love our neighbor with all our
heart, effectively in deed, can bring an increase in grace, a
new outpouring of the Holy Spirit, a growth in divine love.
Since the Holy Spirit is our mutual love—the Father's and
ours—he is being poured abundantly into our hearts by the
Father in our very act of pouring him out in effective love of
neighbor. (Not that we give the Holy Spirit to others, but
that our charity is a participation in the Holy Spirit, it is our
love and his.)

Nor is the communion in the Trinity experienced merely
as communion with one's fellowmen. To those who love one
another, thus keeping the new commandment, Jesus promises a direct experience of the three divine Persons: "If a
man loves me, he will keep my word"—my new commandment to love one another as I have loved you—"and my
Father will love him, and we will come to him and make our

home with him" (Jn. 14:23). Such a one will *know* the Spirit (*ibid.* 17), and Jesus will *manifest* himself to him (*ibid.* 21).

"Written on tablets of human hearts": Spirituality as Sacramental

In our search for personal and Christian authenticity, impelled by the love of Christ, we must "interiorize" these invariables of Christian spirituality. All of them need to be deeply impressed into our consciousness and conscience so that we will live true to what we are by the grace of God. They must be "written not with ink but with the Spirit of the living God, not on tablets of stone but on tablets of human hearts" (2 Cor. 3:3).

The Spirit does this especially through the word and signs of the liturgy, and above all through the preaching of the Gospel. For the word and sacrament are power and Spirit. Both word and sign are intended to impress deeply into our consciousness and conscience what the grace of the liturgy intends to accomplish in us. For the grace granted by the Spirit and power working through the word and sign imposes a responsibility. The word and sign speak to the conscience: "Become what you are through this grace, live true to it. This grace is life—live it! Live it in the way signified in this word and sign."

The word and sign, then, help to bring to explicit consciousness what the paschal Christ wills to accomplish in us by the grace of the sacraments and by our action carried out in the responsibility of that grace. To the extent that our consciousness is alive to this grace, the grace impels our conscience to the corresponding Christian action.

We must therefore write these things in our hearts; for the

Spirit engraves them deeply there only through our efforts to engrave them there; that is, his work in our hearts requires our alertness and openness to him in love and faith, not only in the actual reception of a sacrament but in our continuing pondering in our hearts what the word and sign have spoken to us.

We see, then, one of the chief reasons for the sacramentality of Christian spirituality. Our spirituality, our participation in the life of God, is God's work and ours. His work in us is begun through sacraments—words and signs which signify to us the responsibility which comes with the very grace they give. The words and signs signify to our conscience what God's grace wills to accomplish through our responsible action.

The grace of the sacraments—a participation in the very life of the Trinity—is really too big for human words and signs; and yet, if this divine life is to be incarnate in human action, it needs to be conveyed to us in a human way. And this is done in the divine and human community, the Church, which itself is a sacrament or sign—a visible embodiment—of the communion in the life of the Holy Trinity. Especially in the liturgy is this divine communion of men visibly "bodied forth."

Only a word of preaching which is aflame with divine love will be an effective sacrament of love, only a community aflame with interior love in the Holy Spirit will, through the liturgy, deeply impress the message of grace and love in the hearts of the participants. Community faith and love are ingredients, as it were, of the sacraments through which the Christian community, acting as one with its Head, bestows the grace of the Holy Spirit.

An alert Christian conscience will therefore take great care to try to be "in the Spirit"—wide awake to the Spirit and open to him—in all participation in the sacraments, whether as a minister or as a recipient, or as the praying Church praying for both recipients and ministers. For example, the faith and loving prayers of the "bystanders" at a baptism or at the anointing of the sick will make the sacrament more effective both as sign and as instrument of grace. They are no mere bystanders; they are "sacraments" or expressions of the faith and love of the Church which are essential to every sacrament.

Similarly, the fruitfulness of eucharistic participation can be increased through the mutual love and concern and the prayers of the participants for one another. The priest, for example, as he administers a sacrament, should make that administration an ardent prayer for each individual who comes to him for the sacrament. Or those waiting in line for confession or communion or confirmation should be praying fervently for each individual in turn as he receives the sacrament.

For the communion of the saints, the People of God, is the sacrament of grace and love, and through their mutual love God wills to give love; that is, the Holy Spirit. For Christian love—*agape,* charity—is a participation in the Holy Spirit himself.

Summary

We may unify all the characteristics or invariables of Christian spirituality in three groups:

1. It is Christological, paschal, filial in the Spirit, and therefore Trinitarian. For in the paschal mystery of Jesus, we go as sons in the Spirit to the Father. Thus we enter into

the very life of the Holy Trinity, enjoying intimate personal relationships with each of the three divine Persons in our daily Christian living. Such is the Christian "communion."

2. It is ecclesial, fraternal, communitarian. Our communion with the Father in Christ and the Spirit is necessarily communion in the Spirit with all the brothers and sisters of Christ, children of the Father. This interior communion with God and with one another in God is incarnate in the visible ecclesial community, an embodiment which must be made in the culture of the times and the place.

3. It is also ecclesial, sacramental-liturgical, apostolic. For communion with the Father in the paschal mystery is given to us by Christ only in and from the community of the Church, which is in Christ like a sacrament or sign and instrument of this communion with God and with one another (*LG*1). It is lived in the Body of Christ, which is "knit together in love" (Col. 2:2) and communicates this love.

"The grace of the Lord Jesus Christ and the love of God and the fellowship of the Holy Spirit be with you all" (2 Cor. 13:13).

Amen!

Part Four

THE MERGING
OF CONSCIENCE AND PRAYER

We declared in our general introduction: Prayer and conscience become so intimately one in their cooperation that the functioning of a rightly formed conscience tends to become ever more truly a prayer, while true prayer works for ever greater purity and clarity and sureness of conscience.

In the remainder of this volume, we shall endeavor to unfold the truth of this statement. What we shall say may be summarized as follows:

Conscience, like prayer, is a function in love's quest for personal fulfillment. Indeed, conscience is the place where we meet God and find fulfillment in communion with him. This search can be successful, this quest carried to completion, only when mind and heart are divinely perfected by faith and charity, and the conscience is purified more and more by the indwelling Holy Spirit.

151

Thus conscience cannot function fully and achieve its ultimate purpose except as a prayer—a quest in faith for the transcendent God, an openness in hope to receive his Holy Spirit in his self-communicating grace, and the gift of self to him in love's response. Faith, hope and charity, and the response in the Holy Spirit, are the basic constitutives of prayer.

Prayer and conscience, then, must work as a team.

15

CONSCIENCE: LOVE'S QUEST

Like prayer, conscience is first of all a quest for personal fulfillment. The workings of conscience are a function in the search for what one needs for his true growth. Man grows toward authentic fulfillment through freely chosen right action. Conscience is the guide in discovering this right action.

The dictate of conscience is a judgment of reason concerning the moral goodness of the action to be taken, declaring that it is good inasmuch as it leads one to what he ought to be. And it contains an obligation to this action. The judgment of conscience declares: This *ought to be done* because it is the action which brings you to what you *ought to be*. It brings you to what you ought to become through your action. Or the judgment declares: This ought to be avoided; it is evil, because it is destructive of what you ought to be.

Source of the Obligation of Conscience

Reason comes to such a judgment because it has made a search, it has engaged in the quest for self-fulfillment. The obligating power of conscience springs from the compelling power of hope which urges man on in this quest for authentic fulfillment. The obligation springs from man's very life and being as a lover who *knows;* for man's natural thrust toward fulfillment works through his will as guided by reason—his will as loving, his reason guiding that love. In the very structure of man, then, there is a built-in drive and obligation to search for fulfillment, and in this search, to follow reason's moral judgment.

As a judgment of reason, the dictate of conscience expresses a truth, the truth of life, the truth of living action, the action which is true and good because it leads effectively to the true hope—what one ought to be. It is the authentic action, for it measures true to one's true self, one's self in the making. The truth declared by conscience is thus uniquely my own, my personal truth, pointing out what is good for me here and now in this situation.

The obligating power of the judgment of conscience thus springs from the thrust of man's being toward his authentic self: what he ought to be.

This is a thrust of his nature and of his will. It is a will for the good which is self-fulfillment. Of its very nature, the will is oriented toward this good, and it wills it of necessity. It can choose any other good only when this other good seems to contribute to the further good, self-fulfillment.

Thus the obligation of conscience springs from the moral power of the will, it springs from the very nature of the will as a power to love, but to love rightly—that is, according to reason—to love what reason reveals as leading to what one ought to be. The will in its thrust in hope toward the good puts the reason to work to seek the action which ought to be performed to implement this quest for authentic fulfillment. And the very power of life which impels the will toward this fulfillment obligates it to follow conscience—that is, the dictate of reason indicating what ought to be done.

Conscience: Urge to Authenticity

Conscience is thus the innate urge of the spiritual person—the knowing and loving person—to be authentic, to be true to self. It is an expression of the natural impulse of the person to preserve self as a person by acting in freedom according to one's nature as a person; that is, according to a will guided by right reason. To act contrary to conscience is to destroy one's wholeness as a person, and the gnawing of conscience is the pain of this injury to personal integrity.

So deeply structured into man's very nature is this urge and obligation to act according to reason that when he fails to do so and thereby sins he "fakes" reason, he seeks fictitious reasons to make his action appear reasonable. This kind of "rationalizing," this seeking for plausible but untrue reasons for conduct, this pretense at following conscience, manifests again that it is man's very nature to act according to conscience, the moral judgment of reason.

Deep down, then, the obligating power of conscience is really the drive toward authentic self-love, it is the natural thrust of the will in hope and love toward true fulfillment, it is the urge to be true to self by being true to right reason. Conscience is not a tyrannical power outside us forcing us. It is a love and hope, rightly ordered by reason, springing from the deepest thrust of our personal being.

Conscience and the Transcendence of Self
in Love

In fulfilling this role, says Vatican II, conscience discovers that its basic law—a law which it has not given to itself—is the law which is fulfilled only in love of God and neighbor (*GS* 16). The élan of love which is the binding force of conscience is discovered to be a drive toward a self-fulfillment which can be achieved only in a love which transcends self by loving others. Authentic self-love is possible only in loving God and fellowmen.

For authentic man is he who lives in communion with God and with his fellowmen in relationships of mutual love. Toward this the whole élan of his being impels him, to this his conscience obligates him. To go against this conscience is to work toward self-destruction.

Thus, if the obligating power of conscience is rooted in the will's built-in drive toward the fulfillment of self, conscience as a function of reason and love discovers that self reaches fulfillment only by transcending self, by going out to others in the gift of love.

How does conscience discover the law of love of others? Through love's intuition of reality itself, through reason's reflection upon the ontic structure of mankind as made by God. In making man in the way he did, God "built into" man that law which he detects in the depths of his conscience, "a law which he does not impose upon himself, but which holds him to obedience" (*GS* 16). In its search, conscience accepts the truth it finds. In enunciating its judgment, "This ought to be done," it pronounces a word it has "heard" from God, a word from God which it has read first of all in the very nature of mankind and the person's own being.

For man's first word from God is written in the ontic structure of man and is found through reason's reflection upon man, impelled by the will's search for meaningful action. That is what St. Paul means in saying: "When the Gentiles . . . do by nature what the law requires . . . they show that what the law requires is written in their hearts" (Rom. 2:14–15).

"Heart," in the Semitic thinking of St. Paul, designates the seat of decision, the moral conscience. When it is right, of its very nature the heart gives rise to action according to nature, action regulated by reason which finds its norm for action in human nature and righteous culture.[29] By intuiting human nature and evaluating cultural development, conscience discovers the law of right action and obligates to it.[30]

In this process, "in a wonderful manner conscience reveals that law which is fulfilled by love of God and neighbor" (*GS* 16). In a variety of concrete situations, conscience is able to read this law of love and righteousness written into the ontic structure of mankind. For example, it sees the law of

[29] We add the word "righteous" because human culture can be warped by sin (cf. *GS* 11).

[30] No individual man's reason can discover all this by himself; it is the collective intuition and reasoning of a group of people which discovers in nature itself the law of right action. Vatican II speaks of this continuing collective search in conscience made by mankind (*GS* 16).

love in the truth of self as a person needing others and needing to be loved by them: and able to love in return, able to respond to their love and their need by giving self in return. Thus conscience discovers that the law of love driving toward self-fulfillment is simultaneously the law of love as giving to others.

And in the very nature of things it discovers the ontic relationship of self and of all mankind to Someone who transcends them all, Someone of whom all are in need, Someone to whom all must respond in love's self-giving.

All of this happens when man's heart is right, when his conscience functions as it should. If modern man is not being led by his conscience to love of God and neighbor, it is because he is not really listening to conscience. He does not interiorize his experience of himself and of the world of men and things in which he lives. He does not reflect; he lives too much on the outward surface of his being, in the area of sensation. His whole life is like an explosion outward, his life's forces are scattered in every direction as he allows himself to be attracted almost exclusively by what he experiences outside himself.

He does not return enough to his heart, to the interior of his being, to evaluate, in the light of the whole of his life's experiences, the phenomenological reality which he daily experiences. And not returning to his heart, he does not find God who awaits him there.

The Higher Norm of Conscience

Though we have shown how natural conscience can discover in man's nature and in righteous cultural development what ought to be done, we do not maintain, as do so many of our contemporaries, that the ultimate norm of conscience is merely cultural or social custom, we do not say that man's obligation in conscience is nothing more than to do what is in accordance with his social milieu, for his own welfare and that of his social group.

Social and cultural custom is indeed one of the norms of conscience, and the common good of all is certainly one of the intermediate goals achieved through man's living according to conscience. In our next chapter, however, we shall show how every dictate of conscience is a word from God, and in following conscience man lives in communion with God. Each time we embrace God's will as indicated by conscience, we encounter God himself. Thus the ultimate norm of conscience is God's salvific will, inviting man to communion with him. This communion is granted, for example, on condition that a man is right with his fellowmen, and rightness with our fellowmen is regulated, in no small degree, by right cultural and social customs.

Since its goal is communion with God, mature conscience not only seeks and finds God's will expressing the *conditions* for this communion but, above all, is alert to the intimate personal call to this communion through faith and interior grace. Here again we see how conscience, in its deeper purpose, functions ever more fully as prayer.

Vocation: Definitive Law of Conscience

When man is faithful to his natural conscience which discovers the law of love, he is open to hear the call of divine grace. The call of God, the call of individual divine vocation addressed interiorly to the heart of each man, becomes the definitive law of conscience. If the basic law of conscience is a word from God written in human nature itself, the higher and definitive law is the unique personal word of vocation spoken to each man in his heart.

This, of course, is always spoken within the framework of the basic law of nature, which it does not abrogate but brings to a transcendent perfection. For grace does not destroy but perfects nature. The call of grace is a call to transcend nature (indeed it belongs to the nature of man to transcend himself); it is an invitation into the divine life, a vocation to personal communion with the Father as a son in the Son.

Thus the call of grace to conscience is a call to "build a future" based upon divine hope, a call to seek conscientiously in faith to know more fully "the hope to which he has called you . . . the riches of his glorious inheritance in the saints, and what is the immeasurable greatness of his power in us who believe" (Eph. 1:18–19). It is a call to act thenceforth in this power of God, taking action in hope to become what we ought to be—what God's call and grace intend we should be.

Conscience: Love's Freedom in Responsibility

As a drive toward authentic self-fulfillment, through relationships of love with others and above all with God, conscience is something very positive. Primarily, it points out positive action to be taken, action which expresses and builds love. Only secondarily is conscience a judge of actions already performed, and therefore only secondarily does it give rise to fear by witnessing to guilt. Its first and most ordinary function is to point out the ways of love. When it accuses of guilt, it is simultaneously appealing for a conversion to the ways of love through correction of one's loveless ways, it is calling for the acceptance of God's redeeming love and justifying grace.

Conscience, then, is ever oriented toward love: toward a healthy self-esteem and toward love as a gift of self to others. It bears witness to man as made in the image of the God of love and is love's appeal from the God of love, calling for a return of love in all one's actions.

Thus, even though it is an obligating power, conscience is not in opposition to love but points out the right implementation of love. In its more mature development, conscience experiences its "obligation" rather as "vocation" to love; and understands sin as the refusal to love.[31]

The obligating power, therefore, is not a pressure from without. For the law of conscience—though man does not give this law to himself—is not something alien to him imposed upon him from outside himself; it is the radical movement of his deepest being orienting him in love to God and neighbor. It is an expression of his natural drive toward communion with God and his fellowmen. The deepest laws of being, witnessed to by conscience, are the laws of love. "Love is the fulfilling of the law" (Rom. 14:10).

By its very nature as a drive toward love—responsible love, love guided by right reason—conscience is free. Love cannot be forced; it is given freely or else it is not love. Action according to conscience is love's freedom exercised in responsibility.[32]

[31] L. Monden, *Sin, Liberty and Law* (New York: Sheed and Ward, 1965), p. 9.

[32] See Paul Hinnebusch, "Religious and the Liberty of the New Law," *The Signs of the Times and the Religious Life* (New York: Sheed and Ward, 1967), pp. 78–84.

Formation of Conscience through Love's Interiorization of Law

Since the basic law of conscience is its own interior élan of love guided by right reason, there is no opposition between conscience and law. For conscience interiorizes all other laws, making them its own. Enlightened reason recognizes objective law as good, for it sees that it corresponds with human nature and cultural development and expresses love, the ontic law of all reality. Therefore, reason and will interiorize objective law, accepting it in love as their own law, their subjective personal guide to love, for it is seen to express love's deepest natural thrust toward good, toward personal good within the common good of all in right relationships.

It is exceedingly important, then, that reason be instructed and enlightened in this way. For if it is to function properly, conscience, or reason's natural power to make a moral judgment, needs to be enlightened by knowledge of the objective moral law. The formation of right conscience requires the interiorization of law, the personal grasp of the true good pointed out by the law. Only thus can freedom of conscience be exercised as a responsibility. So that it can be exercised in full responsibility, the faculty of conscience is obliged to search for this truth which is to guide it in its practical decisions.

Contemporary man is uncomfortable with the word "obligation" since to him it connotes pressure from without, and he wants to be free to act from within, in keeping with his dignity as a person acting in knowledge and love. He prefers the word "responsibility" to "obligation." The word "responsibility" is meaningless, however, unless it is seen as the loving, willing interiorization, the personal understanding and acceptance, of ontic obligations, of objective laws built into the very nature of things, laws orientating them toward their authentic fulfillment. One is fully responsible and free only when he makes the objective law his personal interior law through an understanding acceptance of it as true and good, and then freely, lovingly, responsibly acting accordingly.

To maintain that there are laws built into the very nature of man and of cultural development is by no means to deny that man is also by his very nature openness to the future, to the unexpected, openness to grace and the Spirit of God. The objective moral law, built into man's nature, orientates him to God, and it is only in observing it that man is fully open to God. "In all his activity a man is bound to follow his conscience in order that he may come to God, the end and purpose of life" (*DH* 3).

Cooperation of Consciences

In the accurate discovery and acceptance of the objective or ontic law built by God into human nature and developed in human culture, no man can work alone. It is a task for the consciences of all men working in cooperation.

In fidelity to conscience, Christians are joined with the rest of men in the search for truth and for the genuine solution to the numerous problems which arise in the life of individuals and from social relationships. Hence, to the extent that correct conscience holds sway, persons and groups turn aside from blind choice and strive to be guided by the objective norms of morality (*GS* 16).

In other words, conscience must carry on a continuing search for the true action, for the action which corresponds both to man's deepest nature as orientated to love and to the situation at hand. Since it is a united search, a search in which no man can be successful alone, one man's conscience should readily accept helpful guidance from the consciences of others:

Truth is to be sought in a manner proper to the dignity of the human person and his social nature. The inquiry is to be free, carried on with the aid of teaching or instruction, communication and dialogue, in the course of which men explain to one another the truth they have discovered, or think they have discovered, in order thus to assist one another in the quest for truth. Moreover, as the truth is discovered, it is by a personal assent that men are to adhere to it (*DH* 3).

This is the personal assent we have called "interiorization," making the truth one's own in understanding and love. When the moral principles which have been discovered by the cooperation of the consciences of many men have been interiorized by the individual, his conscience will make more accurate judgments and his progress toward authentic fulfillment will be more secure.

When conscience presents an action as good and true, then the will should embrace it in love's free choice. For only when love follows the guidance of enlightened conscience is the natural élan and freedom of love exercised with responsibility. Only by making the right choice under the guidance of rightly formed conscience is the power to love free of the slavery of false love and channeled effectively into the right paths of love.

Thus, action according to right conscience is love's action

exercised in responsibility—in responsibility to self, to one's fellowmen, to God. It is action in enlightened love, action according to the fundamental law of being, the law of love.

Such conscientious, responsible action is the sign of authentic self-love, for only such action is true to self, true to what self ought to be, namely, a person acting out of rightly guided love, and through this action growing toward authentic fulfillment in relationships of love with God and fellowmen.

16

CONSCIENCE:
WHERE WE MEET GOD

In his quest in conscience for self-fulfillment, man discovers that he himself is not the ultimate norm of this fulfillment. For he finds that to fulfill self he must transcend self, he must go out of self by giving self in love. He finds fulfillment only in unselfish relationships with others in love; and indeed, only in the relationship with the Other, God. Conscience is the place where we meet God.

For, as an invitation to transcend self, to measure true to a norm outside self, the dictates of conscience are truly an invitation from God's love to open self to him and his love. To him who faithfully accepts and acts upon the invitations of conscience God always gives himself in love. Thus the quest in conscience, when it is followed with responsibility and fidelity, successfully finds communion with God. As the power by which we achieve communion with God, conscience is truly the faculty by which we pray effectively.

These truths are suggested by Vatican II when it declares: "Conscience is the most secret center of man, *the sanctuary in which he is alone with God,* whose voice resounds in his deepest heart" (*GS* 16). "*Alone with God*": no other man, no creature whatsoever, can get into a man's conscience to force him to do anything. There man is free, there he acts by choice "from the heart." Conscience is the power to love wisely under the guidance of reason; and therefore not even God forces conscience; for no one, not even God, can force love. God *awaits* man in his conscience, says Vatican II.

"By reason of his interiority man surpasses the whole universe of things; he returns to this profound interiority when he turns to his heart, where God, who scrutinizes all hearts, awaits him" (*GS* 14).

Conscience is man's very heart, his "most secret center," in the sense that it is his very essence, that which makes man really man and superior to the whole universe of things. He surpasses all things because, as a person, he can meet God and live in communion with him. He can be with God precisely because he has this "heart"—heart in the biblical sense as seat of moral decision, source of intention, choice and action, power of love and dialogue and communion. "Keep your heart with all vigilance, for from it flow the springs of life" (Prov. 4:23).

In this heart God awaits man, he awaits him in every single act of conscience, he invites him to turn to him in love's choice. Every dictate of conscience is an invitation from God's love, each dictate when accepted and carried out in love brings communion with God in love. Thus every

deliberation of conscience contains promise of an encounter
with God.

Man Meets God Only in the Heart

Though God is everywhere, it is *only* in the heart, the conscience, that he meets man.

God is present at the very ground of man's being, ever
upholding him by his creating power and presence, just as
he is ever upholding all other creatures. But God is where
man is in a far more wonderful way than simply as the power
giving him being. He is there with man at the very roots of
his life, at the heart whence springs man's specifically human
life, the life of love and choice. He is there as the "jealous
Spirit" (Jas. 4:5), in eager love awaiting man's choice of
him, expecting man's communion with him.

Long before man becomes aware of this, and indeed from
the very instant of his creation, the watchful Spirit of love
is there preparing man for the light and invitation he will
offer him, he is there lovingly readying him for the call to
communion. Vatican II expresses it thus:

The basic source of human dignity lies in man's vocation to
communion with God. From his very origin man is already
invited to converse with God; for he exists only because he is
created by God's love and is constantly preserved by it. Nor does
he live fully according to truth unless he freely acknowledges that
love and commits himself to his Creator (*GS* 19).

Nor does the Lord ever abandon man, whom he has made
for himself. "Man, incessantly aroused by the Spirit of God,
will never be altogether indifferent to the problem of religion" (*GS* 41). "God yearns jealously over the spirit which

he has made to dwell in us" (Jas. 4:5). He gave man a spirit so that it could receive the divine Spirit. He gave man the light of intelligence, he gave him a heart from which spring thoughts and desires and intentions, so that man could use it to find his Maker:

He made from one every nation of men . . . that they should seek God, in the hope that they might grope after him and find him. Yet he is not far from each one of us, for in him we live and move and have our being (Acts 17:26–28).

Groping for God

Why is it that man must grope for God like a man in the dark, if God is so near to him, if his love is ever there with him giving him life and movement and existence?

It is because God is not perceptible to man's senses and intelligence in the way that creatures are. God is not just another thing among his creatures who can be found in the way that they can be found. He is totally "other," he is completely transcendent, infinitely surpassing ordinary understanding, even though he is closer to man than man is to himself.

God therefore reveals himself to man in signs, signs which hide him even as they reveal him, signs which can be misinterpreted as well as rightly interpreted. Precisely because he infinitely surpasses human understanding, God cannot reveal himself except by veiling himself under signs.

For those who have eyes to see, all the universe is a sign of the presence of God—"who makest the clouds thy chariot, who ridest on the wings of the wind, who makest the winds thy messengers" (the signs of your presence) (Ps. 104). Though some men can see God in all these things, other men are blind to his presence because they see these things only as they are in themselves, and not as signs of something within them. For such men, creatures hide God rather than reveal him; "they became futile in their thinking and their senseless minds were darkened" (Rom. 1:21), for they have refused the God whose appeal to their consciences was conveyed to them through these things: "for although they knew God (in the things that have been made—Rom. 1:20), they did not honor him as God or give thanks to him" (Rom. 1:21).

Thus the very signs which reveal God to men of right and good heart hide him from the hard-hearted, the men of calloused conscience. And yet, conscience cannot be destroyed, and men who refuse to acknowledge God are nonetheless really groping for him, for they are made for him. The very gnawing of conscience, we said, is nature's protest against the inauthenticity of action which rejects God, action which is untrue to man's self as made for communion with God.

We Meet God only in the Conscience

Though God is everywhere, we said, he meets man only in the conscience, he addresses the signs of his presence only to the heart, the source of love and choice. For by these signs he intends to say much more than the fact that he exists. The signs are always an invitation from a God who desires communion with men. His purpose is always to invite man's love, to elicit man's choice of him, so that in him man might find life.

When the dictates of conscience are maturely understood as an appeal from divine love, then their summons—the "ought" which they involve—is a call which love cannot resist, an invitation which love freely accepts in joy. The response to conscience comes fully from the heart.

In the heart, then, God awaits man's response. Conscience ever says, "You ought to respond, for this is the way to love and life. If you refuse, you will not find life and love and fulfillment. 'Today, if you shall hear his voice, harden not your heart' " (Ps. 94:7, d).

Since God created us in love precisely that he might call us in love, prayer is always a response to this appeal of God to the heart. I pray to God only because somehow God has first spoken to me.

And if I pray appealing to God's mercy and love, inevitably I hear in my conscience the imperative to do the will of God if I wish to be in communion with him in love.

My deep sense of responsibility for becoming what I ought to be (which is what God wants me to be, and what I therefore want to be in love for him) hears the word of his will as a summons of love, an irresistible call of love to love.

Any conscience which does not act in this way is not yet rightly and adequately formed. Such a one has not yet sufficiently contemplated God's love for him personally, he has not yet opened himself enough to receive the fullness of the Spirit of love. His conscience is not functioning with full maturity. We shall return to this point when we consider how the natural thrust to self-fulfillment needs to be perfected by supernatural motivation in charity inspired by the Holy Spirit.

The Hidden Encounter in Conscience

Whether a man knows it or not, it is always God who speaks to him through conscience. Conscience has a voice, but it does not speak its own word, it speaks only the word of God. Even the man who does not know God hears the word of God through conscience. For conscience, we have seen, is reason and love's intuition discovering and declaring how things ought to be; or more specifically, discovering and declaring in the light of reality how this particular man ought to be and to act in this situation. Conscience considers reality and judges and declares man's right relationship to the ontic order. But this order, built into reality itself, is a word from God, a manifestation of the Word by whom all things were made, and through it God speaks to the conscience of man.

Therefore the man who follows right conscience can truly be in dialogue with God and in communion with him even before he is aware that there is a God. For the incomprehensible God speaks to him in signs, and in sincerity and willingness he can respond in a right choice without even realizing that this dictate of conscience is a sign or word from a personal God inviting his love.

Thus he can have a hidden encounter with God. When he responds to the right order revealed to him by conscience and acts accordingly, he is really responding to a sign and invitation from the hidden God, he is becoming his authentic self in relationship with God though he may not even know God, at least not on the level of explicit consciousness. Such a one is called a "latent Christian," or an "anonymous Christian."

When he does this (and he can do it only by a grace of God), God in turn responds to him and gives him the grace of justification, destroying original sin and giving him access to God. Of course, if such a choice in conscience is to bring him the grace of justification, it has to be in a matter serious enough to require a man to go out of himself in the gift of self-sacrificing love. It has to be a fundamental option giving the right direction to the whole of his life, setting the goal of his life not in himself but in an absolute value, which ultimately—though he may not clearly realize it—is God himself. For the absolute value, such as justice and love, which the man accepts in conscience is a true sign of God himself.[33]

And, of course, the option is made in some concrete life-situation. For example, a man may be in a situation where he is faced with the practical requirements of justice and love toward a fellowman. The ought of conscience says: "You must love your brother in this difficult situation at great cost to yourself." Conscience puts the man under the necessity of choosing between self and the absolute order of justice and love which is the ontological law of all human reality, the real order which requires love of neighbor expressed in justice to him. In accepting this order and acting according to it in this concrete situation, implicitly this man is accepting God, the Author of the order, thereby directing his life to God. On the other hand, if he rejects this order, preferring himself to his neighbor by refusing to express justice and love, he is making himself the goal and center of his life, and thereby is implicitly rejecting communion with God, who had appealed to his conscience through the sign of his neighbor.

When the man accepts the dictate of conscience and implicitly chooses God, he receives the grace hidden in the situation. For in every dictate of conscience, not only does God speak to us, but he offers a gift, a grace of friendship

[33] Cf. Yves Congar, *The Wide World My Parish* (Baltimore: Helicon, 1961), p. 121.

with him, and the grace to do his will. In the example we have given, the man has followed his conscience, preferring justice and love for neighbor to sinful self-indulgence, and has thus accepted a sign from God, an invitation to friendship with him. Therefore God gives him his friendship, he communicates himself to him in interior grace, he puts the man "in the state of grace," though the man may not yet be explicitly conscious of God as Person and Friend.

Such is the traditional doctrine of justification through a basic option in which a man orders his life to the true end in a fundamental response to conscience, without necessarily knowing clearly and explicitly the true nature of that end as God. It is a right choice giving the total meaning to one's existence.

In that basic option, a man has sufficiently interpreted the signs of God appealing to his conscience, and has accepted them in right conscience. And therefore in a gift of grace God gives him the reality which was hidden and offered in those signs, namely, God himself. But the man's possession of the reality still infinitely surpasses his human reason and can be grasped only in faith. The grace of faith is necessarily included in the grace of justification, for only by faith can man be justified.

The grace of faith, an interior light or personal "word" from God, itself infinitely surpasses human understanding, and so a man can have it without being able to conceptualize it explicitly. Thus, for example, a man may have faith in God as his Saviour without knowing about Christ and his redemptive mystery, or even without having clear concepts about God himself (cf. *LG* 16).

This basic option of conscience, through which even a pagan can be justified and set on the way to eternal life, is thus explained in the words of St. Thomas Aquinas: "When a man arrives (morally) at the age of reason, the first thing to which his mind must turn is to deliberate about himself, and if he directs himself toward the true end, grace is given him and original sin is remitted."[34]

Doubtless our present idea of personality, and our knowledge of psychological and moral life as a continuous flux, will lead us to see this arrival at the age of reason and deliberation about oneself as consisting, not so much in a single explicit act, as in a progressive unfolding of our deepest attitude toward self, others, life, the moral and spiritual Absolute. Analyzed in this sense, the bearing of the passage remains the same; it is in every way decisive.[35]

Conscience as an encounter with God is thus first of all at a far more fundamental level than the ordinary choices of daily life. It is a basic option which justifies man (or puts him on the way to condemnation). The ordinary daily choices in conscience from then on should be but the expression, the deepening, of the fundamental option for God.

All acts of right conscience require a measure of self-sacrifice, of self-discipline. Whenever a man follows conscience, transcending self in self-sacrifice, choosing God in preference to self, God meets him with a grace of still more intimate communion. Certainly any conscience-situation which calls for a choice which is really costly to self contains an offer of increase in grace and growth in divine love. God waits in the situation, as it were, ready to grant the grace to love in the measure required for making the costly sacrifice. In following conscience, one lays hold of this grace, one acts in

---

34 *Summa Theologica*, Ia–IIae, Q. 89, a. 6; cf. Q. 109, a. 3.
35 Congar, *The Wide World My Parish*, p. 101.

the power of this grace, one receives a new mission of the Holy Spirit and thus grows in divine love in carrying out the action dictated by conscience. Real growth in love of God accompanies any choice in conscience requiring notable self-sacrifice for love of God.

17

THE MERGING
OF CONSCIENCE AND FAITH

According to St. Paul, sincere faith and mature conscience so merge into each other that the words "faith" and "conscience" practically become synonyms. Paul even substitutes the word faith for conscience: "Whatever does not proceed from faith is sin" (Rom. 14:23). And in a passage in which he sums up the duties of a bishop—"The aim of our charge is love that issues from a pure heart and a good conscience and sincere faith" (1 Tim. 1:5)—the words "pure heart," "good conscience" and "sincere faith" are interchangeable. "All stress the absolute limpidity of the spotless soul which gives itself wholly to God and neighbor."[36]

When the word of God is preached, it is always addressed to conscience: "By the open statement of the truth we would

[36] Ceslaus Spicq, *Agape in the New Testament,* II (St. Louis: Herder, 1965), p. 389.

commend ourselves to every man's conscience in the sight of God" (2 Cor. 4:2). For God's word always has an imperative quality about it; it is a summons, an "ought." It is a call for action, for a response in life. It must be lived.

But the fountain of man's living action is the heart, the conscience, the source of love's decision. God's word is a call appealing to the heart, for the response to it must be given freely.

This paradox of simultaneous obligation and freedom is thus expressed by Vatican II: "God calls men to serve him in spirit and truth, hence they are bound in conscience, but they stand under no compulsion. . . . Man's response to God in faith must be free. . . . The act of faith is of its very nature a free act" (*DH* 11, 10).

In fact, human freedom finds its fullest perfection only in response to the word of God. "You will know the truth, and the truth will make you free" (Jn. 8:32).

God always respects a man as a person, he deals with him only as a being whom he has created free: "When God in the beginning created man, he made him subject to his own free choice" (Sir. 15:14, c). "Free" and "person" can almost be used interchangeably.

Person as Freedom

For freedom is personal response to another person. The person by its very nature is open, ordained to completion and fulfillment by transcending self through communion with other persons. Person, as openness, is capacity for relationships in knowledge and love. These relationships, this communion, can exist only where there is a self-revelation, a word of love to another, and a response by the other in a similar self-communication in love.

Only he who stands open to others in receptivity and willing response is fully a person, truly free, existing in personal relationships in love, responding to the word and self-giving of others, giving his own word and self in return.

Man's fullest freedom and personality is accomplished only in the gift of self in response to the Word of the divine Person, God's self-communication in love. Thus is established communion between God and man, and man's freedom is fulfilled.

Hence the necessity of faith, in which alone, in this life, can God's word be received. This word of love, we said, is addressed to man's conscience or "heart." And "to obey it is man's very dignity" (*GS* 16); for he is a free person and God always deals with him as such, God awaits him in his heart, awaits his love's response. He never forces man in any way, for love cannot be forced. Only love is fully free.

Thus, conscience is free. And love has a conscience. Love is constrained, "obligated," to respond to love. And the greater the love on either side, the greater the loving obligation.[37]

The Word: Alive in the Conscience

Addressed to the conscience and received by the conscience, the word of faith should ever be alive in the conscience as a source of life in response to God's love: "Hold the mystery of faith with a clear conscience" (1 Tim. 3:9). Conscience is called faith (Rom. 14:23) inasmuch as it holds onto the word

[37] See Hinnebusch, "Love's Inner Binding Force of Conscience," *The Signs of the Times and the Religious Life,* p. 71.

of faith and acts according to it. For faith is its light, and the word of God received in faith gives it direction. Man must ever direct his life according to the Gospel of Christ; his conscience, perfected by faith, judges how the Gospel ought to be applied in life's particular actions.

For conscience is in vain unless through faith it reaches God in all of life's action. And faith is in vain unless it is operative through conscience in every life-situation. Only each man's personal conscience can judge, in the light of faith, what is good or evil for him personally in this or that precise situation. "Whoever knows what is right to do, and fails to do it, for him it is sin" (Jas. 4:17).

Conscience is therefore immature unless it lives constantly by faith. For only through a conscience fully enlightened by faith can the faith become operative in the whole of life. Only through a conscience expert in "practicing the truth in love" does the grace of God received in faith flow into all of life (Eph. 4:15).

For every grace brings a responsibility. Grace is fully effective only through responsible action carried out in this grace. Thus the grace we receive from God in faith becomes our responsibility in conscience. Through the workings of right conscience, grace effectively passes into one's whole life. Faith and conscience thus work as one.

When conscience thus makes the grace of faith operative in the whole of life, the whole of life is a prayer, a communion with God, a response in grace to God and his grace.

The Heart: Seat of Moral Decision

St. Paul's merging of faith and conscience is fully within the biblical tradition concerning conscience. In the Bible, conscience is always related to God as the hearing of his word, the acceptance of his will, the consciousness of one's relationship to him and responsibility before him. God's saving will is ever the imperative guide of life and action.[38]

The Old Testament, we have seen, rarely uses the word "conscience," but refers to the reality of conscience by calling it "the heart." The heart is the source of thought and love, of word and action; from it spring intentions and moral decisions giving rise to word and deed, for which man is held accountable to God.[39] *"Out of the heart* come evil thoughts, murder, adultery, fornication, theft, false witness, slander. These are what defile a man . . ." (Mt. 15:19). Speech, too, springs from the heart, and therefore we are accountable to God for every word, as for every action: "Out of the abundance of the heart the mouth speaks . . . I tell you, on the day of judgment, men will render account for every careless word they utter" (Mt. 12:34).

The Heart: Wellspring of Life

The conscience is described in Proverbs as the very origin of life, for from it springs all of life's truly human action. Therefore it must be looked after with great care:

> Keep your heart with all vigilance;
> for from it flow the springs of life (Prov. 4:23).

The heart is a source of life only when it receives the word

---

[38] See "Conscience," *Sacramentum Mundi: An Encyclopedia of Theology,* I (New York: Herder and Herder, 1968), p. 412.

[39] Ceslaus Spicq, *Theologie Morale du Nouveau Testament,* I (Paris: Gabalda, 1965), p. 44.

of God and acts accordingly. For the exhortation to guard one's heart carefully is preceded by an exhortation to receive the word of God:

> My son, be attentive to my words;
>> incline your ears to my saying.
> Let them not escape from your sight;
>> keep them within your heart.
> For they are life to him who finds them
>> and healing to all his flesh (Prov. 4:20–22).

The words of wisdom are life, the heart is the spring of life. One truly *lives* only when his conscience responds to the words of God. For the whole context of this passage (Prov. 1–9) makes it clear that the words of wisdom in question are the words of God. Personified wisdom, which dominates these chapters, signifies God's wisdom given to men. "Happy the man who finds wisdom. . . . She is a tree of life to those who grasp her" (Prov. 3:13, 18). Only God's wisdom gives life to man, the refusal of his word brings death. Man lost life—he was expelled from the garden containing the tree of life—when he disobeyed the word of God.[40]

Thus the heart or conscience is made for God; to it God is ever addressing his word of love, which is accepted or rejected. When it is accepted and carried out, man lives! His right response to the word brings him into communion with God; he lives in the divine presence, in God's Garden. His rejection of the word, however, cuts him off from God and from life; for life is communion with God.

[40] These ideas are treated in detail in Hulsbosch, *God in Creation and Evolution,* especially Chapters 4 and 5.

Conscience Is Transcendent

Thus conscience is always a relationship with God. By its very nature it is transcendent openness, receiving its word from beyond itself and "carrying man across" to someone beyond himself.

For though conscience is a voice, it does not speak its own word, it speaks only what it hears from God. And the word which it hears and speaks is always a call to man to transcend himself, to go out of himself to God, to find his fulfillment not in self but in communion with his Creator and Redeemer.

Since its word is not its own, right conscience is ever a hearing, an accepting, an obeying. It functions fully and maturely only as faith; for we have seen how the man who follows conscience when faced with the necessity of making a basic life-decision receives from God the gift of divine faith and justification. And divine faith is always at least implicitly faith in Christ and his paschal mystery. Man can transcend self and achieve the communion with God to which conscience calls him only by the grace of faith which must thoroughly enlighten his conscience and become one with it.

Conscience: a Quest in Faith for the Transcendent God

A conscience fully and permanently right can exist only in that faith. And faith is itself, by its nature, a search and a hope: a search which is certain that it is on the right way, and a hope which is firmly confident of success: "Faith is the assurance of things hoped for, the conviction of things not seen" (Heb. 11:1).

As a quest for deeper understanding and as a confident reaching for things not yet fully possessed, a living faith is ever a prayer, a stretching out for fuller communion with God.

Thus conscience too can function with fullest maturity only as a prayer, as a quest in faith for the transcendent. Life as a quest and a progress toward something completely transcending man and his powers cannot achieve its purpose except by the power coming to it from God, the grace received from him in faith and hope. Only a conscience enlightened by faith, and functioning in hope and love, can make this power and grace of God so operative in life that life's quest is successful.

If conscience is to function fully as faith, the word of God must ever be alive in man's heart, it must ever be in the forefront of his consciousness, not buried and forgotten, driven out of mind and heart by a multitude of other concerns. Only frequent explicit prayer and regular listening to the word of God, and loving pondering of the word in the heart, can insure that our conscience will ever function in full maturity as faith operative in life, faith working in love (Gal. 5:6).

18

THE SPIRIT OF WISDOM
IN OUR "HEART OF HEARTS"

Divine faith, we said, is always at least implicitly faith in Christ. It is always the redeeming Word that speaks to man's conscience—even when the message comes to him through creation, or through his own nature, or in a life-situation, or in some other way. For only in the Redeemer and his paschal mystery can any man have communion with God. Therefore, conscience can achieve its ultimate purpose only through implicit and explicit faith in Christ and through the indwelling Spirit of Christ, who alone can purify the heart of man.

These truths are reasserted by Vatican II. "The Holy Spirit in a manner known only to God offers to every man the possibility of being associated with this paschal mystery" (GS 22). "They too can attain to salvation who through no fault of their own do not know the Gospel of Christ or his Church, yet sincerely seek God, and *moved by grace* strive

by their deeds to do his will as known to them through the
dictates of conscience" (*LG* 16). Even those without explicit
knowledge of God "who *by his grace* strive to live a good life"
will not be denied the helps necessary for salvation (*LG* 16).

The grace working in these men, says the Council, comes
from Christ; "it is given by him who enlightens all men so
that they may finally have life" (*LG* 16). Thus in "all men
of good will in whose hearts grace works in an unseen way"
(*GS* 22), Christ is at work, for he is the Head of all men
without exception. The risen Lord personally exercises his
action of grace, offering his Holy Spirit, fruit of his paschal
mystery, to every man.

To say that God awaits every man in his conscience is to
say that the redeeming Word awaits him there, desiring to become the indwelling light of that conscience, desiring to pour
his purifying Spirit into that heart.

Therefore, the most impelling of all responsibilities in
conscience is the acceptance of Christ and his word: "I have
come as light into the world that whoever believes in me may
not remain in darkness. . . . He who rejects me and does not
receive my sayings has a judge: the word that I have spoken
will be his judge on the last day" (Jn. 12:46, 48). Every sin is
implicitly a rejection of Christ.

The rejection of his word plunges us into darkness. Sin has
the effect of blinding man; tainted by sin, a man can easily
deceive his own conscience. "He sees himself with too flattering an eye to detect and detest his guilt" (Ps. 36:2, j).

Every man's heart is more or less tainted and darkened by
sin, either his personal sin or original sin, the sin into which
he is born. "The heart is deceitful above all things, and desperately corrupt; who can understand it? I, the Lord, search
the mind and try the heart" (Jer. 7:9–10). Every man's heart

needs the light of Christ to show it to itself. The Lord who knows every heart confronts man with his sin in order to save him.

This, we have seen, is always the first task of the word of the Lord: it pronounces judgment upon man's heart, it challenges every conscience, manifesting its thoughts and intentions.

"Teach me wisdom!"

Confronted by the Word of God, the revealing Light, the sinful heart of man is called to conversion by the same Word which manifests its sinfulness. He who accepts this call to conversion cries out like the psalmist: "God, create a clean heart in me. . . .

"Since you love sincerity of heart, teach me wisdom in the secret place," the deepest depths of my heart (Ps. 51:10, 6, j).

"Sincerity of heart" and "wisdom," presented here in Hebrew parallelism, are practically synonyms. When the thoughts of a man's heart are right and sincere, they are wisdom, giving rise to life which is right and true. Ordered to living action, wisdom or sincerity of heart is a dynamic quality; a sincere heart is the flowing fountain of wisdom springing up to true life.

Man's Need of a New Heart

Only the Holy Spirit of God can grant this wisdom to the sinful heart of man: "Create a clean heart in me, do not deprive me of your Holy Spirit" (Ps. 51:10, j). Because "the heart is deceitful above all things and desperately corrupt" (Jer. 17:9), God finds it necessary to give man a new heart.

"A new heart I will give you and a new spirit I will put within you. . . . And I will put my Spirit within you and cause you to walk in my statutes and be careful to observe my ordinances" (Ezek. 36:26–27).

Therefore, admitting he was born in need of a new heart and of God's spirit—"you know I was born guilty, a sinner from the moment of conception"—the psalmist cries: "God, create a clean heart in me, put into me a new and constant spirit, do not banish me from your presence, do not deprive me of your holy spirit" (Ps. 51:5, 10, j). Just as man's heart is light only when God's "eye" or light is in it, so his spirit is right and sincere only when God's holy Spirit is in it; only then does it have the wisdom impelling to true life.

The justification of the sinner is the most wonderful of all the works of God and is analogous to the act of creation: "*Create* a clean heart in me." The verb *create* is used in the Scriptures only of God; he alone can do it. So, too, he alone can give a new heart to man, he alone can set right the sinner.

Indeed, the Holy Spirit has to go to the very deepest roots of man's life to set him straight there. When Proverbs cautions us to guard our heart because it is the source from which life springs (4:23), it tells us to receive the words of wisdom into our "heart of hearts" (4:21, a), the deepest roots of our life and action. So, too, the psalmist prays: "Teach me wisdom in the secret place," the deepest depths of my being, the radical source of my life (Ps. 51:6, j).

The New Testament calls this creation of a new heart in man a rebirth. In fact, the Hebrew word *bara,* create, really means "to beget as sons." Our Lord speaks of the justification of the sinner through faith and baptism as being "born again of water and the Holy Spirit" (Jn. 3:3, 5), in whom we cry,

"Abba, Father!" The Spirit, purifying our hearts at the deepest source of life, dwells in "the heart of hearts" as himself the source of life. He is the "living water welling up to eternal life" (Jn. 4:14; cf. 7:38). "God's love has been poured into our hearts through the Holy Spirit which has been given to us" (Rom. 8:5).

Only through a living faith in Christ, the redeeming Word, can our consciences be alive in the Holy Spirit; for they have been purified in baptism through the shedding of the Blood of Christ and the power of his resurrection: "The Blood of Christ who through the eternal Spirit offered himself without blemish to God (shall) purify your conscience from dead works to serve the living God" (Heb. 9:14). "Baptism is a pledge made to God from a good conscience through the resurrection of Jesus Christ" (1 Pet. 3:21, j).

Our conscience always needs the presence of the indwelling Spirit of God, who alone sets our heart straight and keeps it from sin, filling it with wisdom and purifying it ever more by the power of the resurrection: "My conscience bears me witness *in the Holy Spirit*" (Rom. 9:1). He alone is our infallible guide: "All who are led by the Spirit of God are sons of God" (Rom. 8:14). "Teach me to do your will, for you are my God. May your good spirit guide me on level ground" (Ps. 142:10, c).

Élan in the Holy Spirit

The Spirit is not merely a guide but gives to our heart a divine élan of love. For the wisdom of the Spirit is no mere knowledge; it is love's dynamic drive toward righteous living action. When God gives us a new heart and a new spirit by the gift of his Holy Spirit, he gives us "the wisdom of the

Spirit" (Rom. 8:6, d), in contrast to the false "wisdom of the flesh" (*ibid.*), which is hostile to God. In translating Romans 8:6 in this way, "The wisdom of the flesh is death, but the wisdom of the Spirit is life and peace," the Vulgate seems to have appreciated St. Paul's awareness of the biblical concept of wisdom as a dynamic élan of true life. The false "wisdom," that of the flesh, is also a dynamic thrust—toward death. Romans 8:6 is thus translated in the Revised Standard Version: "To set the mind on the flesh is death, but to set the mind on the Spirit is life and peace."

This drive in the Spirit toward right action, toward life and peace, is thus subject to our acceptance of it, our setting our mind on it, our docility in receiving it, our cooperation in freely and responsibly making it our own. For the Spirit never forces our conscience, he awaits us in our heart. He offers his light and love, his grace awaits us in every situation of conscience and becomes ours when we make our decisions in humble openness to his help.

And yet, to say that the Spirit *awaits* us in our heart can be misleading, especially when we are speaking of the fully committed Christian. The really fervent lover of God has given self so totally to the Holy Spirit, in such loving eagerness to be entirely Christ's, that the Spirit no longer has to await, as it were, this Christian's consent. He knows that he will eagerly accept *whatever* God asks, whatever he inspires.

In such a one, totally surrendered to him, he works as he pleases, taking the full initiative, arousing ardent acts of love for Christ and the Father which come forth from the heart with amazing spontaneity. A mere look at the crucifix, a mere word from the Scriptures, and the man of the Spirit "sighs his soul" toward the Lord who is Love.

In such a one, likewise, the Spirit inspires heroic works in the service of mankind. To him he gives the insight to renew the Church, to change the world, to solve the insoluble problems of the times. Till we have more such "men of the Spirit," Christians of our time will continue to "run aimlessly," to "box as one beating the air" (1 Cor. 9:26), to thrash about helplessly like a fish out of water, in all sorts of insecurity and identity crises.

The more we live according to his light and love, the stronger becomes in us his élan of love toward true life, the "spring of water welling up to eternal life" (Jn. 4:14). His Spirit and ours merge more and more, as it were, into one spirit: "He who is united to the Lord becomes one spirit with him" (1 Cor. 6:17).

Hence St. Paul's frequent exhortation, "Be renewed in the spirit of your mind and put on the new nature" (Eph. 4:23). The creation of a new heart called for by the psalmist, the creation of the new man begun in baptism, is a continuing process which goes on through our response to the word of God as he speaks to our conscience in a multitude of ways. Only through a conscience formed daily according to the Word of God and in the light and love of the Holy Spirit does the grace of baptismal renewal pass effectively into our whole life. "Be renewed in the spirit of your mind and put on the new nature . . . which is being renewed in knowledge after the image of its Creator" (Eph. 4:23 with Col. 3:10).

Part Five

"BE RENEWED
IN THE SPIRIT OF YOUR MIND"

The natural impelling power of conscience, we have seen, is love and hope seeking fulfillment. But only in the wisdom of the Spirit, the élan of love springing from our "heart of hearts" where he dwells, can we come to life and peace in God, where alone we find fulfillment.

The remainder of this book will deal chiefly with our co-operation with the Holy Spirit as he purifies our heart and renews us in the image of our Creator, fashioning us in the likeness of Christ, the Authentic Man.

19

LOVE'S INSIGHT AND DECISION

Love is blind, they say. They say this when someone marries a very homely person, or a scoundrel. "When your heart's on fire, you must realize smoke gets in your eyes."

But is love really blind? In truth, love is very perceptive. Love has eyes to see what no one else can see. Beneath the plain features or the ungainly body, love sees a person, the image of the lovable God. Or in the scoundrel love sees a human being who perhaps can still be redeemed by love and patience. True love, moreover, has a wonderful power for understanding the beloved, for seeing his needs and knowing how to care for them. Thus a mother's love knows instinctively what to do in her child's need.

The only love which is really blind is egoism, selfishness. The self-centered person, interested only in self, has no insight into the needs of others and no ability to care for them. In self-love, moreover, the egoist is blind to his own shortcomings. "He sees himself with too flattering an eye to detect and detest his guilt" (Ps. 36:2, j). He is not very perceptive in understanding and carrying out God's will for his sanctification. Sin, the refusal to love, the rejection of the dictates of conscience, causes a blindness, a darkness which makes it increasingly difficult for a man to see the light.

Only a conscience filled with the Holy Spirit of love can break through the blindness of egoism and selfishness and sin. For true love does have eyes to see; and the divine love inspired in our hearts by the Holy Spirit can see the deep things of God!

While it is still weak, of course, even true love has little insight. Love which is still mixed with selfishness is blind to the extent that it is selfish. But great love has wonderful insight.

Therefore St. Paul prays "that your love may abound still more and more in knowledge and all discernment for approving the better things; that thus you may be sincere and blameless unto the day of Christ, full of the fruits of righteousness which come through Jesus Christ, to the glory and praise of God" (Phil. 1:9–11, s).

Christian love, then, has eyes to see. But it needs to grow in this insight, this discernment, this perception of God's true will. In short, love has a conscience, but it needs to refine this conscience more and more. Love's eyes must become ever more enlightened to see what is to be done to please God, to be blameless before him and to produce the good fruits of the Christian life.

We hear incessant talk these days about love, professedly in protest against legalism and confining structures. Love is the only law, it is enough to love.

But not everyone who says, "Love, love," will enter the kingdom of heaven, but he who does the will of the Father who is in heaven. "Knowledge without love," says St. Bernard, "puffs up—but love without knowledge strays into error."

We must take care, then, to acquire love's true insight, we must daily refine our consciences so that we can discern ever more clearly God's true will for us, and carry it out with firm decision. True conscience does not claim as right only what seems good to one's own judgment, rejecting all external norms, but is ever impelled by love itself to make a painstaking search to discover God's true will.

Hence St. Paul tells us: "Do not be conformed to this world but be transformed by the renewal of your mind, that you may prove what is the will of God: what is good and acceptable and perfect" (Rom. 12:2).

For the Christian as for the Jew before him, the norm of morality and spirituality is the salvific will of God. Love is not a law unto itself. Love has to have insight to discern the will of God.

Therefore, St. Paul is constantly praying for his converts, that "having the eyes of your heart enlightened" (Eph. 1:17), "you may be filled with the knowledge of his will in all spiritual wisdom and understanding" (Col. 1:9).

The Virtue of Decision

St. Catherine of Siena, great lover of St. Paul that she was, had a special predilection for this power of love to discern. She calls it the virtue of discretion, describing it at great length in her Dialogue.

For most English-speaking people, unfortunately, the word

"discretion" connotes only "cautious reserve"; it has lost its vigorous positive meaning. Not so for St. Catherine. For her the word discretion always carries its full dynamic meaning of "power of free decision, of personal choice."

Discretion, in Catherine's thinking, is love's insight leading to love's right and firm decision. Discretion, she teaches, grows out of love. It is a main branch on the tree of charity. It is love's eyes, love's clear perception; it insures that love will express itself in the right and just way. It guarantees that we "practise the truth in love" (Eph. 4:15, c).

The love's discretion of which St. Catherine speaks is Christian prudence. Unfortunately, the word prudence, like discretion, means for many of us nothing more than cautious reserve. In its full meaning, however, prudence is a dynamic power for making right and firm decisions and carrying them out. The prudent person is the one who gets things done— the right things. He fulfills love's responsibilities. Prudence, for St. Paul, is love's insight, fruitful in the works of righteousness (Phil. 1:9–11). St. Catherine calls it love's discretion. Thomas Aquinas describes it as "prudence, love choosing wisely."[41]

But perhaps we should call it the virtue of decision, for prudence gives clear insight into what love should do in response to God's salvific will, makes a firm decision to do it, and does it. One's conscience is mature only when it is perfected by the virtue of decision.

St. Catherine of Siena not only *spoke* about love's discretion, she practised what she preached. Discretion, enlightened decision, "was perhaps the distinctive trait of her

---

[41] *Summa Theologica*, IIa–IIae, Q. 47, a. 1, obj. 1.

spiritual physiognomy."[42] She always showed imaginative
boldness in her projects, along with extraordinary courage
and unshakable assurance in carrying them out. She always
knew what she was about, and why. A woman of right decision and sure execution, she was the kind of person sorely
needed in our times of indecision. Hers was the creative
action of which the contemporary theology of hope speaks
so much. Whenever she encountered a situation marked
with sin, she always took positive action, in the power of the
risen Christ, to redeem it.[43]

A mother's love, we said, instinctively understands her
child's needs, and swiftly, surely does the right thing in caring for them. Likewise, Christian love, as it grows stronger
and purer, grows also in love's insight into what is to be
done, and goes about doing it with firm decision. Without
insight and decision, love remains empty, lacking truthful
expression in works pleasing to the Beloved, or it makes
foolish mistakes which offend God and injure our fellowman.

Love's Clear Conscience and Christ the Truth

For love's action must ever be in conformity with the truth.
So that we will "no longer be children, tossed to and fro . . .
according to the wiles of error," says St. Paul, "we are to
practise the *truth* in love, and so grow up in all things in
him who is the head, Christ" (Eph. 4:14–15, c). The words
"practise the truth" are very rich in connotation; St. Paul

[42] A. Lemonnyer, *Notre vie spirituelle à l'école de Sainte Catherine
de Sienne* (Juvisy: Editions du Cerf, 1934), p. 76.
[43] See below, Chapter 23, "Redeeming the Time."

means that we should accomplish the truth, express it in our
lives, profess it by living it, showing it forth. We are to do
this in love.

Love cannot live in a haphazard way; love must live *the
truth.* "The truth" is love's norm of morality, the truth is
the guide of love's conscience.

But precisely what is this truth? St. Paul speaks of it in two
ways. Sometimes he indicates that the truth to be lived is
Christ. At other times he says that the truth to be lived is the
will of God. But the salvific will of God has its clearest expression in Jesus Christ. Thus St. Paul is saying the same
thing in two different ways when he says to the Romans, "Be
transformed by the renewal of your mind that you may prove
what is the will of God" (Rom. 12:2), and when he says to
the Ephesians and the Colossians, "Be renewed in the spirit
of your mind and put on the new man . . . one that is being
renewed unto perfect knowledge 'according to the image of
his Creator' " (Eph. 4:23; Col. 3:10, c).

For God's salvific will intends to restore us in his own
image and likeness. Jesus is the image of the Creator who is
the pattern of the restoration. He is the "image of the invisible God" (Col. 1:15). That is, in Jesus the unseen God
is made visible as the pattern of our life. Thus Jesus,
authentic man and image of God, is the full expression of God's will for us, the pattern to whom we are to
conform our lives, the truth whom we are to profess in love.
For he *is* the truth—only in him do we measure true to what
we ought to be. "Therefore be imitators of God, as beloved
children, and walk in love, as Christ loved us and gave himself up for us, a fragrant offering and sacrifice to God" (Eph.
5:1).

The task of love's discernment, then, the task of Christian

conscience, is to perceive the truth of Christ in every life-situation and carry it out with firm decision. The task of love's conscience is to translate the truth which is Christ into love's living action in the here and now, thus "redeeming the time" (Eph. 5:16, d)—redeeming our personal lives and the world in which we live by living the truth of Christ in love, thus carrying on the work of Christ's redemption in our lives and in our times.

We see again why St. Paul can call conscience faith (Rom. 14:23), for the task of the Christian conscience is to translate the truth of Christ, accepted in faith, into love's daily actions. The Christian ought to direct his conduct according to "the law of Christ" (Gal. 6:2), and his conscience judges how this law can be applied in such and such a particular situation.

Conscience as Daily Decision for Christ

Christian conscience thus puts the faith into action in all of daily life; it is a power of daily decision for Christ. When we first come to believe, we decide for Christ; but through an enlightened conscience, with ever deepening insight, our love translates that initial decision into all of our living. Each decision made by right conscience is a renewal and deepening of the original commitment. We not only *decide* for Christ by following conscience, we *live* Christ. Through conscience we translate the grace we receive from our Head into living action as his members.

Thus again we see the relationship of conscience to prayer. Our entire life is a lived prayer to the extent that it is an acceptance and implementation of God's will in every situation of life. But this can be done only by a rightly formed, fully enlightened conscience, translating faith and love into everyday life. Conscience in its perfect functioning is practically a prayer, for like prayer it is love's response to the call of God's word—his personal word to me.

We "pray always" when "the eyes of our heart are enlightened" (Eph. 1:17), so that our love is "filled with the knowledge of his will in all spiritual wisdom and understanding" (Col. 1:9), and we "practise that truth in love" (Eph. 4:15), carrying it out with firm decision.

How exceedingly important, then, is the spiritual insight which guarantees that our love will not be blind and will not remain in the realm of mere talk, but will be translated into deed and *truth*. Let us therefore frequently join St. Paul in his prayer for us: "That your love may become richer and richer and be accompanied with a full knowledge and keen practical insight, so that you may appreciate true values . . . that you may continue to be upright and blameless until the day of Christ, and be filled with the fruit that springs from holiness through the aid of Jesus Christ to the glory and praise of God" (Phil. 1:9–11, k).

20

LOVE'S REVERENCE

Formation for Freedom of Conscience

Contemporary personalistic philosophy rightly insists on the necessity of making personal decisions in full freedom of conscience, breaking loose from unchristian structures and customs which hamper the freedom of the sons of God. Therefore, in the name of freedom of conscience, many people today are declaring their independence of law and social structures; but only too often with disastrous results. For only too many of them have not been adequately educated to make truly enlightened decisions of conscience. They have not formed their consciences in authentic Christian freedom.

Freedom and free will are not exactly synonyms. Freedom is a perfection of the will, a right formation of the will, just as knowledge of the truth is a perfection of the intellect.

Careful formation of the will for freedom is necessary if
personal decisions of conscience are not to be disastrous for
self and for the human community in which we live. Education for freedom is basically this formation of right conscience.

Reverence: the Root of Freedom's Insight

What is the starting point in formation for love's enlightened decision-making? In unison with the Scriptures, St.
Catherine of Siena would answer: "A loving reverence for
God." The virtue of enlightened decision, she writes, is the
main branch on the tree of love of God and neighbor. But
the tree is rooted in humility. Humility, however, is basically
a loving reverence for God. As we have already noted, the
fundamental postulate in St. Catherine's entire spiritual
doctrine is knowledge of self in relationship with God, and
love's acceptance of this relationship.

Humility, however, is not merely the acceptance of the
truth of one's nothingness without God; it is at the same
time a full recognition of the marvelous gifts which He-who-
is has lovingly bestowed upon us. It is the truthful recognition of one's personal endowments, but in grateful and
joyous acknowledgment that all of these are God's gift of
love. One could not even exist if it were not for his gracious
and generous love endowing one with this existence. "I am
he who is, you are she who is not."

Humility, then, is a loving, reverential, grateful acceptance of one's total dependence upon divine love, along with
a generous, trusting gift of self to him for the accomplishment of the purposes of his love. This basic discernment of
one's true relationship to God gives rise, in turn, to clear

insight and right decision concerning every other relationship, in every situation of life. One sees clearly how to render glory to God and love to neighbor, and how to evaluate rightly all of God's creatures.

St. Catherine's living experience of this truth is in total agreement with the testimony of the Bible. The Book of Proverbs teaches that all moral and spiritual insight is rooted in religious reverence for God. Fully enlightened Christian conscience can be based only upon this profound reverence.

The key sentence of the Book of Proverbs is this: "The first principle of knowledge is to hold the Lord in awe" (Prov. 1:7, a). We are more familiar with other translations of this idea: "The fear of the Lord is the beginning of knowledge" (Prov. 1:7, c), "The beginning of wisdom is the fear of the Lord" (Prov. 9:10, c).

"Fear of the Lord" is the Old Testament expression for what we call the virtue of religion. It is religious reverence, loving awe in the presence of the divine Majesty; it includes faith, trust and humble submission to him in love. Isaia says of the Messiah, "His delight shall be the fear of the Lord" (11:3, c). Jesus rejoiced in humble submission to the Father in his paschal mystery, "for the Father is greater than I" (Jn. 14:28). In his prayer in his agony, says the Epistle to the Hebrews, Jesus "was heard because of his reverent submission" (5:7, c).

The fear of the Lord—"to hold the Lord in awe"—is the beginning of wisdom or knowledge. For the author of Proverbs, wisdom and knowledge, as well as understanding and prudence or insight, are practically synonymous. This is because, for the ancient Hebrews, wisdom was insight for right living. It was good practical judgment, it was the ability to

make the right choice and decision. It was rooted in the
reverential knowledge of God, which gives light for right
moral perception.

According to Proverbs, then, the starting point for right
formation of conscience is reverence for God: "The first
principle of knowledge is to hold the Lord in awe" (1:7, a).

The author expands upon this key sentence, telling how
we should be open for this wisdom, earnestly pray for it,
ardently seek it:

> My son, if you will accept what I tell you
>   And will treasure my injunctions,
> With your ears attuned to wisdom,
>   Setting your mind on understanding,
> If you will cry aloud for insight
>   And raise your voice for understanding,
> If you will search for it as men search for silver
>   And hunt it like hidden treasure—
> Then you will perceive what "reverence for the Lord" is,
>   And discover what it means to know God (2:1–5, a).

The author goes on to show how this knowledge of God,
rooted in reverence, leads in turn to clear moral insight and
right decision in life's practical affairs:

> For it is the Lord who gives wisdom,
>   It is he who teaches knowledge and discernment,
> He is the secret of upright men's good judgment,
>   The shield of virtuous lives,
> Guarding the paths of the just,
>   And vigilant for those devoted to him;
> Thus you will come to discern what is right and just,
>   And the way you go will be good (2:6–9, a).

The author continues, showing how this enlightenment—God's gift which has been prayed for and eagerly sought—will dwell, as it were, in one's mind and heart:

> For wisdom will enter your mind
>   And knowledge will be a joy to your spirit,
> Discretion will become your mentor
>   And understanding your protector (2:10–11, a).

This is a foreshadowing of St. Paul's magnificent teaching that the Holy Spirit, absorbed, as it were, into our spirit, enables our spirit to discern rightly the will of God (Rom. 12:2), so that we can "live the truth in love" (Eph. 4:15; cf. 3:16f.).

The author of the Book of Proverbs is content to state categorically the facts about the source of moral insight. We moderns want to grasp the psychological reasons behind the facts. Let us consider briefly some of the reasons why loving reverence is the foundation of right conscience, why loving awe is the beginning of love's true insight and right decision.

Reverence: Antidote for Egoism

Reverence for God leads to true insight because it brings us out of our egoistic blindness. Our acts of free choice are always situated within "the way we are"; we choose what seems to correspond best with what we are and what we desire in love. Thus all our judgments are conditioned by what we love. If narrow self-love is predominant in us, our judgments of conscience are colored accordingly. We see everything from a narrow, selfish point of view; we tend to rationalize as right and good whatever forwards our selfish desires. The eye in us is darkness (Mt. 7:23).

But loving respect and concern for others tends to bring us out of self and corrects our view of things. Loving reverence for God is the best corrective of all.

And what is reverence? Reverence is a mixture of awe and love in the presence of a person of overwhelming goodness and majesty. Because he is good, we are drawn to him in love; because he is overwhelming in greatness we are humble and respectful before him. Loving reverence for the majesty of God—"the fear of the Lord"—is a powerful antidote for self-centered blindness; for our love is drawn away from self-centeredness toward his astounding goodness, and our eyes are opened wide to *his* loves and *his* concerns, especially his fatherly concern for our brothers and sisters, a concern which we make our own. "The beginning of wisdom is to hold the Lord in awe" (9:10, a).

This is why Catherine of Siena can say that humility, reverence for God, makes possible right decisions in regard to both God and neighbor. Humility is essential to righteousness.

Reverence and Love's Enlightened Consideration

Even between human beings there is no true love without reverence, without humility before one's fellowman—a deep respect for his person, a concern for his dignity, a sympathetic understanding of his viewpoints and desires, an alertness to his well-being, an ability to detect his needs and prompt decision in caring for them.

This reverence for the person of each of our fellowmen expresses itself in a tactful sense of the appropriate in all our relationships with him, a delicate, sympathetic perception of what is considerate and what is pleasing. Love knows, for example, when to welcome someone graciously with heart-warming conversation, but it knows also when to respect his privacy, leaving him to his need for solitude and reflection. Love is not forever chattering.

This tact and insight, this openness to understanding what is the fitting thing to say or do, comes from love's esteem of the other's worth as a person, love's reverence for his value as the image and likeness of God. Respectful love is never blind.

Loving reverence for God, then, and loving reverence for neighbor are the best guarantee for right judgments of conscience. Reverence destroys blinding egoism and clears the way for love's perception. Reverential concern for neighbor is loving reverence for God himself: "I tell you solemnly, in so far as you did this to one of the least of these brothers of mine, you did it to me" (Mt. 25:40, j). "He who withholds kindness from a friend," says Job, "forsakes the fear of the Almighty" (Job 6:14).

The more deeply we reverence our fellowmen, the freer we become of egoism, and so the more open we are to the experience of God in prayer. And the more deeply we experience the holiness of God in prayer, the deeper is our insight into the sacredness of our fellowmen and of all God's creatures.

The teaching of Proverbs concerning reverence and insight is confirmed by St. Paul's analysis of the blindness and moral stupidity in the pagan world of his times, and the resulting degrading sins against neighbor. "They became futile in their thinking and their senseless minds were darkened" because, "although they knew God, they did not honor him as God or give thanks to him" (Rom. 1:21). The failure to reverence God in their manner of living gave rise to increasing moral darkness and all kinds of sins against one another (Rom. 1:26–32).

Pope Pius XII said, "Irreverence is the besetting sin of our times." Pope Paul VI, while still Cardinal Montini, wrote a pastoral letter on this loss of the religious sense, the losing of the sense of the sacred, which characterizes our times. This contemporary irreverence for the holy is no doubt at the root of the increasing darkening of the moral sense in western civilization.

The moral blindness described by St. Paul is sin's own punishment, and the disastrous state of affairs it leads to is called "the wrath of God." By this, St. Paul does not mean anger in God; the wrath of God is the punishment, the disorder, which man makes for himself by his moral stupidity (Rom. 1:18). Proverbs had spoken of sin as its own punishment (Prov. 4:19; 5:21–23, a), and in a long passage, Wisdom personified warns:

> Since I have called and you have refused to listen . . .
>   I in turn will laugh when sudden calamity strikes you . . .
> When panic strikes you like a sudden squall wind,
>   And disaster falls on you like a gale,
>   When distress and anguish come upon you.
> Then men will cry out for me, but I will not answer.
>   They will seek for me but will not find me.
> Because they showed no love for knowledge
>   Nor any wish to reverence the Lord . . . (Prov. 1:24–29, a).

Only a restored reverence for the sacred will guarantee the right insights which will save us from disastrous decisions of conscience. Vatican II issued a strong document calling for freedom of conscience; and it is right and just to encourage personal decisions in full freedom in every possible way. But

such freedom cannot be enjoyed without right formation of
conscience. And the starting point toward this is "to hold the
Lord in awe."

> Trust in the Lord wholeheartedly
>> And do not rely solely on your own intelligence;
> Recognize him in whatever you do
>> For it is he who will keep your paths straight.
> Do not pride yourself on your wisdom,
>> Revere the Lord and avoid what is wrong—
> This will bring health to your body
>> And give fresh life to your bones (Prov. 3:5–8, a).

For wisdom "is a tree of life to those who take hold of her;
fortunate are they who hold her fast" (Prov. 3:18, a).

21

MATURITY—IN THE SPIRIT

The beginning of wisdom is to hold the Lord in reverence. Expanding this basic thought, the author of Proverbs declares: If you seek wisdom ardently, cry out for it in prayer, open yourself for it in reverence and humble docility, you will receive it—for it is the gift of God. Wisdom will enter and dwell in you like a permanent and delightful guest:

> Wisdom will come into your heart
> And knowledge will be a joy to your spirit (Prov. 2:10).[44]

These words, we said, foreshadow a wonderful teaching of the New Testament. As we grow toward Christian maturity, St. Paul tells us, the Holy Spirit becomes ever more com-

[44] First line, Revised Standard Version; second line, Anchor Bible.

pletely absorbed into our spirit, so that we become ever more, as it were, "one spirit with the Lord" (1 Cor. 6:17). We acquire "the mind of Christ" (2:16), that is, Christ's way of seeing things, his manner of loving, his practical insights and judgments, his kind of decisions. We receive "a secret and hidden wisdom of God" (2:7); we penetrate "even the deep things of God" (2:10); we become ever more completely "men of the Spirit" (2:15), endowed with a keen practical insight to "judge all things" (2:15).

St. Paul presents these magnificent statements between two references to the immaturity of the Corinthians. "It has been reported to me," he says, "that there is quarreling among you, my brethren" (1:11). The Corinthians are torn by dissensions because of their swelling pride over imagined wisdom. Therefore, Paul gives a discourse on the true wisdom; namely, the foolishness of the Cross. He ends his treatise by referring again to the divisions among the Corinthians, which he now gently brands as immaturity—you are babies, he says, you are still carnal (3:1–2). "For while there is jealousy and strife among you, are you not of the flesh, and behaving like ordinary men" (3:3) rather than as sons of God?

Between these two references to the immaturity of the Corinthians, Paul tells us what Christian maturity is. Or rather, we arrive at Paul's concept of Christian maturity by analyzing his explanation of why the immature Corinthians are blind to the true wisdom.

Paul is pointing out why the divine wisdom he preaches fails to penetrate into the hearts of these men, even though they are "in Christ" (3:2)—and by the expression "in Christ" Paul means that they have been baptized, they have been incorporated into Christ. They have received, he says, "the Spirit which is from God" (2:12)—which is another reference to their baptism. But, Paul complains, they are still "babies in Christ" (3:2). And this immaturity is their own fault. For when he first came to preach to them, it was to be expected that he should feed them on milk. But by now they ought to be ready for solid food, a deeper possession of divine wisdom.

If, then, they are in Christ, and have received the Holy Spirit, why are they not *acting* like men who have the Spirit? Why are they still carnal like ordinary men? Why aren't they spiritual men? Their lives are a paradox—they are spiritual men and they are not spiritual men. They are spiritual in the sense that they have received the Holy Spirit in baptism, but they are mere carnal men in the sense that they are not acting according to the Spirit.

All Christians ought to take these words of Paul to heart; we should seriously ask ourselves: Are we too, like the Corinthians, acting like mere human beings, or are we men and women of the Spirit, living fully according to the Holy Spirit granted us in baptism? There is our real Christian challenge: to be really spiritual people, people ever impelled by the Holy Spirit. The signs of Messianic days, said the ancient prophets, would be the outpouring of the Holy Spirit upon all the People of God, not just upon a chosen élite. Just because the Holy Spirit is in us, just because we are in a state of grace, it does not necessarily follow that we are what St. Paul would call men of the Spirit, spiritual men. But *all* Christians can and ought to be spiritual men, not mere ordinary men like these baptized but immature Corinthians. There ought to be no culpable immaturity in our lives.

Divine Wisdom for All

Because the men to whom Paul was writing were not acting according to the Spirit, the divine wisdom offered by Paul did not penetrate into their hearts. "We impart wisdom among the mature," he says, ". . . a secret and hidden wisdom of God" (1 Cor. 2:6). Obviously, he tells them, you are not mature; your uncharitable dissensions prove this.

In what sense is the wisdom he brings "secret and hidden"? Does he mean that it is a wisdom reserved only for a tiny élite among the Christians? By no means! This wisdom of the children of God is really intended for every Christian, for every one who is "in Christ." It is only "the world" that cannot receive it. It is not "a wisdom of this world," says Paul, "nor of the rulers of this world, who are passing away" (2:6, c).

"This world which is passing away" is a phrase used by Paul more than once to signify the old order of things in contrast to the new creation in Christ (cf. 1 Cor. 7:31). The baptized—they who are in Christ, they who have received the Spirit—are the new creation (2 Cor. 5:17; Gal. 6:15), and the wisdom which Paul brings by his preaching is meant for all of them. Only the world cannot receive this divine wisdom; that is, they who are not in Christ because they have deliberately rejected him.

Why, then, are these Corinthians blind to this wisdom, even though they have been baptized in the Spirit and are "in Christ"? It is because of their defective attitudes, it is because of the obstacles they have placed in the way of the Spirit who dwells in them. It is because they are acting like babies; and their bickering is the sign and fruit of their immaturity.

Maturity: Complete Openness to the Spirit

If these dissensions are the fruit, what is the deep root of
their immaturity? It is their failure to be fully open to the
Holy Spirit, who leads us to maturity; and this, of course, is
due to their unmortified pride, their egoistic selfishness. It
follows then that maturity, in Paul's thinking, is complete
openness to the Holy Spirit. The carnal Christian acts like
an ordinary man, the spiritual Christian is the one who is
totally surrendered to the Holy Spirit, having mortified his
proud selfishness.

St. Paul's sentence "We impart wisdom among the mature,"
then, does not refer to a necessarily small and élite group of
Christians; "rather it envisages *all* Christians *in so far* as they
allow the divine Spirit to operate and become effective in
them."[45] The Christian deserves to be called a mature "man
of the spirit when he allows himself to be taught the secret
of divine wisdom by the Spirit of God who was given to
him."[46] And this is a practical wisdom, expressed in mature,
everyday Christian living. "The believer must patiently
allow the Spirit of God to teach him the secrets of God
hidden from man's gaze, and this is what constitutes maturity
in faith."[47]

We can say, then, that the whole aim in Christian living is
to come ever more fully under the impulse of the Holy
Spirit, from whom alone we can receive the divine wisdom
—that is, the practical insights from God which make full

[45] R. Schnackenburg, "Christian Adulthood According to St. Paul,"
Catholic Biblical Quarterly (July, 1963), p. 357.
[46] *Ibid.*, p. 359.
[47] *Ibid.*, p. 360.

Christian living possible. The Holy Spirit must be accepted as the full light of our conscience. As St. Paul puts it:

The Spirit searches everything, even the depths of God. . . . No one comprehends the thoughts of God except the Spirit of God. . . . And we impart this in words not taught by human wisdom but taught by the Spirit, interpreting spiritual truths to those who possess the Spirit.

The unspiritual man does not receive the gifts of the Spirit of God, for they are folly to him, and he is not able to understand them because they are spiritually discerned. The spiritual man judges all things, but is himself to be judged by no one. "For who has known the mind of the Lord so as to instruct him?" But we have the mind of Christ (1 Cor. 2:10).

If, then, every Christian must aim for spiritual maturity, and this maturity consists in letting the Spirit work effectively in oneself, it is clear that the basic aim of our Christian endeavor is to surrender ourselves ever more effectively to the Holy Spirit, who is the root of all the fruits of Christian living. If the pride and the dissensions of the Corinthians were proof of their immaturity, signs that they were not rooted in the Holy Spirit, then living according to the Holy Spirit will produce charity and peace and joy among us. "The fruit of the Spirit," says St. Paul, "is love, joy, peace, patience, kindness, goodness, faithfulness, gentleness, self-control. . . . If we live by the Spirit, let us also walk by the Spirit" (Gal. 5:22, 25). That is, if the Holy Spirit, given us in baptism, is the source of our life, then let us live true to the life which is in us. If we have the Holy Spirit, then let us act like it.

This Holy Spirit, to whom we strive to surrender ourselves ever more completely like Mary at the Annunciation, to whom we have to be persistently attentive in thoughtful self-possession, is the source of the love of God in which we cry ever more truthfully, "Father!" and the source of the love of neighbor, in whom we say ever more sincerely, "Brother! Sister!" It is not enough to say this in words; our whole "wisdom" or way of life—has to cry "Father!" and "Brother!" and "Sister!" Dissensions are the sign that we are not in the Spirit.

So then, brethren, we are debtors, not to the flesh, to live according to the flesh—for if you live according to the flesh you will die, but if by the Spirit you put to death the deeds of the body, you will live. For all who are led by the Spirit of God are sons of God. For you did not receive the spirit of slavery to fall back into fear, but you have received the spirit of sonship! (Rom. 8:12-16).

The Foolishness of the Cross: Our Wisdom

This putting to death the deeds of the flesh—which St. Paul says is necessary for living in the Spirit—is the wisdom of the Cross, which he contrasted with the false wisdom of the immature Corinthians. "The word of the cross is folly to those who are perishing," he says, ". . . but the foolishness of God is wiser than men" (1 Cor. 1:18, 25). The Cross was the practical, workable wisdom of the life of Jesus. It has to be the working wisdom of the everyday life of all who are "baptized into Christ" (Rom. 6:3).

Therefore, after listing "the works of the flesh" and contrasting them with "the fruits of the Spirit," Paul says, "Those who belong to Christ Jesus have crucified the flesh with its passions and desires" (Gal. 5:25). It is very important to remember that by flesh Paul does not mean merely the gross sins of the body. "Flesh," in Paul's vocabulary, means man inasmuch as he is subject to the fallen state, the old order of things, whereas "spirit," in contrast, means man inasmuch as the Holy Spirit dwells in man's spirit, renewing and recreating him, integrating him into the new creation in Christ, the new Adam.

So among sins of the flesh, Paul includes sins of the mind and heart and soul as well as sins of the body—he includes pride and envy, discord and ambition, as well as gluttony and lust and drunkenness. When we live the wisdom of the Cross, we crucify these deeds of the flesh, "the old self."

But, says St. Paul, "the wisdom of the cross is folly to those who are perishing." The man who does not live according to the Spirit of God thinks that it is foolish to deny himself the pleasures of pride and vanity and ambition and lust and greed. And they indulge in every pleasure which comes their way, wishing to experience everything.

Our contemporaries think it is especially foolish to surrender oneself to another. They would say, in response to St. Paul's definition of maturity: "You call it *maturity* to surrender self to the Holy Spirit. But I call that foolishness. For is not such a surrender of self a destruction of one's liberty, does it not destroy one's autonomy? And is not autonomy, self-rule, self-possession, liberty, the very essence of maturity?"

The person, however, who does live according to the Holy Spirit, and therefore possesses the hidden wisdom of the Cross, in his divine enlightenment knows very clearly that it is in dying that we live. And he knows that we possess ourselves in freedom only that we may give ourselves in freedom. We possess ourselves in freedom when we give ourselves in love, for freedom is the power to love. Death to selfish egoism frees us from the narrow confines of self so that we are free to love God and neighbor and find fulfillment in love.

It is only by giving ourselves to the Holy Spirit that we come into full possession of ourselves, for he alone gives us to ourselves—by giving us the power to love, the power to break free of narrow egoism in the cry, "Father! Brother! Sister!" the power to be fruitful in charity, joy, peace, patience, kindness, goodness, faithfulness, gentleness, self-control—the fruits of the Holy Spirit.

To hold the Lord in reverence, then, is the beginning of wisdom—the practical wisdom of true Christian living. For in humble reverence for God, one is open to the guidance of the Holy Spirit. And "all who are led by the Spirit of God are sons of God" (Rom. 8:14).

"Since the Spirit is our life, let us be directed by the Spirit" (Gal. 5:25, j).

22

SAYING YES TO GOD

The woman at the well could meet Jesus as God—and not merely as a thirsty stranger or as a prophet—only when she faced up to herself and admitted what she was, a sinner. Only then could she encounter Jesus, in faith and in hope, as her personal Saviour and "Saviour of the world" (Jn. 4:42). She saw her God only when God showed her herself for what she really was.

For the Word of God confronts every man "that thoughts out of hearts may be revealed" (Lk. 2:35), that man may see how he stands before God, that he might be converted and be saved.

But it is not only the total sinner, not only the man in mortal sin, who needs this confrontation with the Lord and with himself. Even the man who is in the state of grace, the friendship of God, often cannot see his God as well as he should because the work of redemption is not yet finished in him. There is still much darkness in him because he is still saying "No!" to God in some area or other of his life. He is not doing God's will in some matters, and he is deceiving his own conscience, presenting it with fictitious reasons to rationalize away his guilt. Prayer is difficult for him, because his conscience is not yet fully purified of these areas of darkness. Man cannot easily meet God in prayer, he cannot live comfortably in his presence, he cannot exist in intimate communion with him, as long as he continues to say "no!" to him in some area or other of his life.

Before he sinned, Adam was fully at ease in the divine Presence, prayer seemed as natural to him as breathing, he walked with the Lord "in the garden in the cool of the day" (Gen. 3:8). But after he sinned, he could no longer face his God. "The man and his wife hid themselves from the presence of the Lord God among the trees of the garden" (Gen. 3:8).

But Adam was hiding as much from himself as from God. He would not face up to his guilt and admit it. He tried to shift the blame onto his wife. He no longer referred to her with affection as "my wife," but called her "the woman you gave me," as if blaming God! "The woman whom thou gavest to be with me, she gave me fruit of the tree, and I ate" (Gen. 3:12). The woman, in turn, shifted the responsibility to the serpent: "The serpent beguiled me, and I ate" (3:13).

Are our prayer difficulties likewise due to our refusal to face up to our sinfulness? Are we still saying "No" to God in some area or other of our life? Is that why we have difficulty in meeting him in prayer? If we cannot seem to come face to face with him, is it because our way of living is not quite right? For we pray the way we live.

If we live in openness to God, hiding nothing from him or from self, not rationalizing away our failings, our approach to God will be sincere and genuine, and we will be open to his manifestations of himself.

The surest way to distort one's conscience and to stifle the Holy Spirit of prayer is to indulge in self-seeking and to rationalize this self-seeking, as though it were not infidelity to the Spirit of sonship in the crucified Christ.

If, then, we want to grow spiritually, we have to be constantly alert to the possibility that we will do this, that we will live according to the old fallen nature rather than according to the Holy Spirit, all the while deceiving our conscience into thinking that all is well and that we are quite holy. We must beware of building up an exaggerated image of our holiness and perfection; we must squarely face up to our sinful self and acknowledge in humility our need of continuing redemption.

For even though the child of God on earth aspires in the Holy Spirit to embrace the heavenly Father, he still remains also a child of Adam in whom the grace of redemption has not yet had its full effect. And therefore the true child of God is characterized by, and kept safe by, the Holy Spirit's gift of filial fear. This gift includes humble willingness to admit one's proneness to selfishness of one kind or another, it includes a healthy fear of the possibility of offending the beloved Father.

An important part of the process of growth in personality and spirituality, then, is learning to accept the *reality* of ourselves as we are, not as the perfect someone we imagine

ourselves to be. We hide from our true self each time we
rationalize in order to get our selfish desires; we deceive ourselves into thinking that these are worthy desires. Each time
we rationalize, each time we find reasons to justify what we
want rather than what God wants for us, we misuse our
conscience, we reject the grace offered in the situation and
the responsibility it brings, we quench the Holy Spirit, we
hide from our true self like Adam hiding from his naked-
ness after he was stripped of grace.

We hide from the deeper-down selfish self which is behind this selfish act which we are rationalizing, and we reject
the better self to which God is calling us, which we could
become in seeking and accepting God's true will in this
situation. We are not redeemed from our selfish self and
raised to our better self, because in not accepting God's will
we close ourself to the saving grace it always offers.

On the other hand, our redemption is being accomplished
in every act of ours which is in accord with a truly mature
conscience, a conscience which seeks always to do the will
of the Father. By each of these acts we are redeemed a
little more from the old self, we are transformed a little
more into the higher existence of the divine sonship to which
the Father is calling us.

Hence the necessity of cultivating, with the help of the
Holy Spirit, an eagerness never to refuse the Father anything, a readiness to "always do what is pleasing to him"
(Jn. 8:29). Only his salvific will, sought and fulfilled with an
alert conscience, will redeem us from ourselves. Such a
conscience, for example, sees his saving will manifested in
a call to obedience; or in a situation calling upon us to
change our own plans in order to come to the aid of some-

one in need; or in the hidden, humble, unglamorous service of our fellowmen; e.g., a mother's service of her children, a teacher's service in the classroom, a nurse's in the sickroom. To an alert conscience, God's will presents endless opportunities each day to die to self and rise to a higher existence in his divine Son.

The rationalizer, on the other hand, who is saying "No" to God but is justifying his refusal, whose workings of conscience therefore are far from being a prayer, is not being daily redeemed from his selfishness but is becoming more firmly enslaved. He who is clever in camouflaging his selfishness even from himself often proclaims, while insisting on having his own way: "My conscience is clear! My conscience is my guide! As a mature adult, I follow it in freedom." But only too often, for such a person, conscience is only a synonym for the false self-image he has set up.

It is well for us to remember that the work of redemption is not yet completed in us and we are still somewhat tainted by sinful tendencies. Consequently, our conscience can still deceive itself. For, as we have seen, our judgments are always situated within our condition, we choose what seems to correspond best with what we are and what we desire. If selfishness is still strong in us, or if we are still in the blindness resulting from our former refusals of the light, then our judgments in conscience will be colored accordingly, and unwittingly perhaps we will deceive ourselves in finding reasons to justify what we selfishly want.

"Lord, that I may see!" (Lk. 18:41; Mk. 10:51). This cry of the blind man of Jericho is recorded by the evangelists immediately after their account of the blindness of the apostles, who could not see how self-seeking they still were

—ambitious (Mk. 10:37), concerned about riches (Mk. 10:26) —and could not see the need of the Cross in their lives (Lk. 18:34). Lord, that we may see how blind we are!

The only way to freedom from this darkness is a consecration of self to the Holy Spirit; that is, a determined will to seek and ask his light day after day, and a determined will to seek always what is pleasing to the Father. Lord, that I may see!

The person who is ever loudly appealing to freedom of conscience in rejecting the guidance of authority or of objective norms had better carefully ask himself: Am I sure that this which I claim is from a dictate of conscience is really from the Holy Spirit, or is it from my unredeemed self? Am I judging according to what I am, a sinner, to whom evil looks good, or according to what I ought to be, according to Christ and the will of the Father?

Freedom of conscience is not freedom to rationalize until we find a fictitious reason to justify what we want. One may justly appeal to his rights in conscience only if he has made every sincere effort to find God's true will in the situation, prayerfully considering all the possible indications of this will.

The son of God, living in the filial fear inspired by the Holy Spirit, faces up to his human condition as being also a son of Adam, not yet totally transformed by grace and still in the process of redemption, and still capable of deceiving his conscience. In humility he is not cock-sure that his conscience is always right, he is not forever loudly appealing to his rights in conscience, but is open in humility to counsel and guidance from his fellowmen, and thus is more open to the Holy Spirit.

A mature and enlightened Christian conscience is one

which prays persistently, for the first point of wisdom is
to know whose gift wisdom is:

I perceived I would not possess wisdom unless God gave her
to me—and it was a mark of insight to know whose gift she was
—so I appealed to the Lord and besought him, and with my
whole heart I said: ". . . Give me the wisdom that sits by thy
throne . . . for even if one is perfect among the sons of men, yet
without the wisdom that comes from thee he will be regarded
as nothing. . . . Who has learned thy counsel, unless thou hast
given wisdom and sent thy holy Spirit from on high?" (Wis.
8:21–9:17).

One's life is a prayer only to the extent that it is directed
by a truly enlightened conscience, a conscience enlightened
by the wisdom from above, by the Father's own Word and
Spirit. Such a life is a prayer, for it is a response to the grace
and word of God contained in each situation of life. Prayer
is always a response to God's word. And conscience receives
this word.

The conscience which ever works as a prayer is more than
a seeking and accepting of God's will in each situation as
it comes along. It presupposes a more fundamental prayer,
a permanent attitude of self-offering, of total availability
to the Lord's will, of openness and readiness for anything at
all the Father asks—a spirit of total consecration to his saving
will and to the Holy Spirit of wisdom.

This steadfast consecration has no preconceived self-image
which admits of no readjustments, it has no permanently
fixed concept of what God wills for us. "My thoughts are not
your thoughts, nor are your ways my ways, says the Lord"
(Isa. 55:8). The spirit of permanent self-offering is ever
ready for the unexpected from God, ready for every indica-

tion of his will no matter how surprising or disconcerting it may be. It embraces every sign of God's will no matter what readjustments this forces one to make in one's plans, no matter what revisions it requires in one's preconceived idea of where one's fulfillment lies. The Christian hope surpasses all understanding. We will never reach the fullness of Christian existence unless we are ready for anything God asks, no matter how disconcerting it may be at first.

If we seek always to do the things pleasing to the Father, if we have a deep-down commitment to him, a commitment springing from the very roots of our being—from there where the Holy Spirit dwells, giving rise to our desires for the Father—we will be able to adapt to anything that comes our way; not without suffering, of course, but always with real growth toward our true self, toward a divine fulfillment in Christ which surpasses all we could ever think of or ask (Eph. 3:20), the fulfillment of children crying, "Father!" "We are children of God, and if children, then heirs, heirs of God and fellow heirs with Christ, provided we suffer with him in order that we may also be glorified with him" (Rom. 8:16–17).

23

"REDEEMING THE TIME"

Part of the process of growing in personality and in spirituality is learning to face reality, coming down out of one's dream world and exaggerated idealism, accepting life as it really is, accepting our fellowmen as they are; above all, accepting self as one really is, not the perfect someone one imagines oneself to be but one still in the process of being redeemed. One must accept the human condition.

We do not know ourself as we ought till we know ourself as in need of continuing salvation, a member of a mankind still suffering from original sin and from the effects of personal sins which ratify and deepen original sin. For the redeeming power of Christ has not yet finished its work, it has not yet thoroughly penetrated our personal being nor the human community in which we live.

We must learn to accept these facts, not resent them. In

humility, we must accept our human condition and that of those around us. Disappointments, frustrations, failures, sins, personal mistakes, disillusionment with our fellowmen —all these are part of the stuff our life is made of.

And we must beware of blaming everyone but ourselves for this situation, as Adam blamed Eve, for by our personal sins we too have ratified the sin of Adam and have deepened the fallen state of our race.

Hope in the Redeeming Spirit

But lest this frank facing up to our human condition utterly discourage us, even more than accepting self we must learn to accept the presence of the redeeming Spirit who has been poured into our hearts by the love of God, the Spirit who gives rise to hope which "is not disappointed" or discouraged in the face of our helplessness and nothingness (Rom. 5:5). We have to be like the "poor of Yahweh" of the Old Testament. Theirs was a spirituality of hope. It was not merely a realistic consciousness of their neediness before God, it was a great hope in the saving God.

And this saving God dwells within us, for he has poured his Holy Spirit into our hearts. In receiving this gift, we were redeemed; and yet, we are still being redeemed. "You were sealed in Christ with the Holy Spirit of promise, who is the pledge of our inheritance until its full possession is redeemed" (Eph. 1:14, s). Our redemption from our fallen state is a continuing process, as the grace of the Holy Spirit penetrates our personal being and our human community ever more thoroughly—if we accept him in humility and cooperate with his purposes.

This is what St. Paul means when he says: "Put off your

old nature which belongs to your former manner of life
and which is corrupt through deceitful lusts, and be renewed
in the spirit of your minds and put on the new nature,
created after the likeness of God in true righteousness and
holiness" (Eph. 4:22–24).

Recognize your old nature, the fallen Adam still in you;
recognize your continuing need of renewal. Accept your
weaknesses, your disappointments, your problems and failures, your difficult tasks and frustrations, and respond to
them in the redeeming power of the Holy Spirit who is in
you. Be renewed from within, by the Spirit of God. Recognize him as the source of the continuation and perfecting
of your redemption. Respond to every situation with op-
timism in the Holy Spirit, the Spirit of promise and hope;
and in his power transform your life, redeem it.

Accepting the Shortcomings of Others

Once we have accepted our own human condition, once
we have faced up to ourself as in need of continuous redemption, we will find it easier to accept with understanding and patience the weakness and failings of those around
us. We will no longer be crushed in disillusionment with
others, we will no longer be inclined to blame everyone
but ourself for our miseries.

We tend to blame our troubles on the persons and the
world about us, as Adam blamed Eve and Eve blamed the
Serpent. The new generation is likely to condemn the generation which brought it into the world. It is prone to resent
those who went before for leaving the world in such bad
shape. The young are easily roused to anger by the imper-
fections of their elders and of anyone in authority, and rise

in rebellion. But only too often those who are loudest in their condemnation of authority are the ones who have not faced up to their own personal weaknesses and will not tolerate weaknesses in others.

It is true that the upset world into which we are born is in its sad state precisely because those who have gone before us have ratified the sin of Adam by their own sins, thus deepening and intensifying original sin, "the sin of the world." And our immediate predecessors, of course, blamed those who went before them, and ultimately all the blame is shifted onto poor Adam, as if the rest of us had no personal responsibility for the continuation and worsening of the mess.

However, our attitude of condemnation and resentment and rebellion can be itself another ratification and intensification of the rebellion of Adam. It is necessary, rather, that we accept the human condition of our fellowmen in compassion. "Let him who is without sin among you be the first to throw a stone at her" (Jn. 8:7). Each stone cast worsens the situation, deepens the sin of the world. We must accept the human condition in compassion, in humility, and in hope in the Spirit, assuming the responsibility for bettering it by the redeeming grace of Christ.

Jesus in the Human Condition

Yes, it is sad and painful to be born into so miserable a world—but it is the world into which Jesus was born, Jesus who embraced his Father's salvific will and accepted the human condition, the miserable situation in which he found himself; Jesus who accepted suffering and betrayal, enmity and persecution, disillusionment with disciples whom he had wished to trust.

Jesus accepted everything he found in the human situation except its rebellion, its "No!" to God. "For we have not a high priest who cannot have compassion on our infirmities, but one tried as we are in all things except sin" (Heb. 4:15, c).

He was the perfect "Yes!" to God. He accepted in every situation the Father's saving will. He saw each miserable situation he encountered as a sign of his Father's will for him, as an invitation to sacrifice himself to redeem the situation, as an opportunity to put to work his redemptive power which could be effective only in self-sacrifice. In every situation he said "Yes!" to his Father's redemptive will.

When, therefore, we do not find a perfect world, instead of resenting it and compounding its rebellion, and condemning everyone in a responsible position because he or she is still too human, still a bit unredeemed, let us recall, rather, our Lord's redemptive acceptance of things. "For God sent the Son into the world, not to condemn the world, but that the world might be saved through him" (Jn. 3:17).

If the world is so imperfect—the world into which God put us as he put his Son into it—we must say "Yes!" to it as a son of God, not "No!" as a son of Satan. We must say "Yes" to the salvific will of God which offers us a grace to transform every situation. "Look carefully then how you walk, not as unwise men but as wise, redeeming the time, because the days are evil. Therefore, do not be foolish, but understand what the will of the Lord is. . . . And be filled with the Spirit" (Eph. 5:15–18).

We must face the reality before us as a sign of what God

wills we should do, as an invitation to sacrifice self to redeem the situation. If the days are evil, it is because we
made them so, and we must redeem them by the grace of
Christ. Experiencing our helplessness and hopelessness in
an evil world, we must face the situation in the hope which
springs forth from our hearts, the hope springing from
the redeeming Holy Spirit who dwells in our hearts.

Starting with our own hearts, we must begin to build a
new world by the redemptive power which is in us. "Be
renewed in the spirit of your minds, and put on the new
nature" (Eph. 4:23). Our new life must grow from the Holy
Spirit who is in us, and from us must spread to others. We
must live in total consecration or availability to the redeeming Spirit, offering ourselves with the prayer: "Lord, make
me an instrument of your peace. Where there is darkness
let me sow light. Where there is hatred let me sow love,
where there is doubt, faith; where there is despair, hope."

Our response to everyone and every problem should be
an expression of the One who dwells in us. The quality or
value of our response to friend or foe, to problem or to success, depends upon how deeply this response is rooted in
the Holy Spirit within us.

Personal Responsibility

No matter what our predecessors in the human race have
done for us or against us, each descendant of Adam and
Eve, by the mere fact that he is a responsible person, has
the primary responsibility for what he makes of his life:

In the design of God, every man is called upon to develop and
fulfill himself, for every life is a vocation. . . . Endowed with

intelligence and freedom, each one is responsible for his fulfillment as he is for his salvation. He is aided, or sometimes im-
peded, by those who educate him and those with whom he lives,
but each one remains, whatever be these influences affecting him,
the principal agent of his own success or failure.[48]

A perfect world, then, is never given to us on a silver
platter. Each one, as a free and responsible person, must
work for his own fulfillment and help build a better world.
Each time we encounter a situation which bears the mark
of sin and therefore cries out for redemption, we should see
it as a sign of God's will that it be redeemed. And, in the
power of the Holy Spirit who dwells in us, responding to
the challenge, we should offer ourselves to God's salvific will,
surrendering ourselves more fully into the Father's hands,
making ourselves totally available for his redeeming work.
Nothing is hopeless in the consciousness of the redeeming
Spirit who dwells in us, in whose light and power we labor
to correct the situation.

Even when it is humanly beyond our power to change
a bad situation, great good still comes out of the situation
when we offer ourselves to the saving will of God, along with
Christ in his sacrifice. Thus, "I complete what is lacking
in Christ's afflictions for the sake of his body, that is, the
church" (Col. 1:24).

Moreover, our self-offering in complete availability to
God's salvific will sets us right with God. As a "Yes" to him,
it helps destroy all those "No's" in various areas of our being
which had set us at odds with him and had made it difficult
for us to experience his presence in prayer. Our "Yes" to
God in each situation helps complete our redemption,

---

[48] Pope Paul VI, *Progressio Populorum.*

freeing us still more from our old fallen self, taking us to God with Christ, bringing us into deeper communion with the Father.

This quickness to offer self to God in complete availability, this spirit of consecration, should be our basic, permanent prayer-attitude. It was the life-long attitude of Jesus. For one can enter into the divine presence—from which Adam and Eve had withdrawn in disobedience— only in the loving obedience of Christ. God meets our self-offering, our openness to him, with a new outpouring of his Holy Spirit.

24

THE COMPATIBILITY
OF AUTHENTIC PRAYER
AND HUMAN SINFULNESS

Most of us, at some time or other, have seen a prayerful person suddenly act in a very unchristian way. Or perhaps it was we ourselves, prayerful though we were, who turned viciously upon our fellowman and did him an injury. This may even have happened shortly after we had experienced a great grace of prayer, or a profound intimacy with the Eucharistic Lord.

What are we to think of the prayer of a person who thus sins against his neighbor? Are we to conclude immediately that it was not prayer at all, but was sheer hypocrisy or self-deception?

Is it not unjust and sinful on our part to brand as hypocrites those who pray assiduously even though they are not yet perfect in their love and service of their fellowmen? Is it right to demand that these people stop praying and approaching the Eucharist until they have overcome all their failings? For some of us have gone to the absurd extreme of condemning all prayer and liturgy and religion simply because many Christians are still imperfect in love. Is it right to condemn prayer just because men of prayer sometimes fall into sin?

And are we wise in abandoning prayer just because we discover that we ourselves have deep-seated faults and sinful tendencies? When through the experience of falling into sin in times of stress we come to realize how weak and sinful we really are, should we therefore conclude that all our previous prayer was only self-deception, and that God had not really been with us? In discouragement over our sins, should we abandon prayer as being hypocrisy? In the desire for authenticity, should we give up prayer as being self-deception, since we are really sinners and therefore not as close to God as we thought we were?

Some contemporary religious have made this mistake. When they experienced their sinfulness through their falls, in spite of years of effort at prayer, they have mistakenly concluded that their earlier prayer experiences were self-deception, and have foolishly repudiated, as fostering hypocrisy, the traditional religious forms of prayer and aids to prayer. "Self-deception" is the name they give to prayer when they find so many faults in themselves in spite of their past efforts to pray, or when they see so much lack of Christian love in others who pray.

To conclude that the prayer of an imperfect man is self-deception, or to call a prayerful man a hypocrite just because in weakness he occasionally falls into sin, is to insult the Holy Spirit of grace and the God of love. For prayer is a gift of God's grace, and it is God who takes the initiative

in prayer, offering the grace of prayer even to sinners and
to the imperfect. Prayer is one of the best remedies for
sinfulness and imperfection, and it is not hypocrisy for a
sinner to pray. The grace of prayer is a call to conversion,
an invitation to turn more deeply to God in love and to
turn away from the ways of sin. It is quite normal, then,
that a person, though still very imperfect in love of neighbor,
should pray sincerely and even experience God in prayer.

But if such a prayerful experience is really a call to conversion and to greater love of God, how can a person possibly
sin against his neighbor soon after praying? If his experience
of God in prayer was truly authentic, how could he possibly
be unloving when he meets his fellowman? If God's presence
and grace was truly working in him in prayer, does this not
mean that God's grace then abandoned him, that he should
sin against his neighbor?

To expect that an authentic grace of prayer should make
us thenceforth totally sinless is like blaming the Holy Spirit
for our sins, as if his grace did not really work. It is like condemning him for not giving us so miraculous a grace that we
could never sin again once we had had some taste of God in
prayer. This is like expecting his grace to make consummate
saints of us in a flash, without our cooperation.

His graces of prayer, however, are a call for our cooperation, they are invitations to greater love on our part, they
are a summons to correct ourselves, an appeal to us to make
the gift of self to God on a more profound level than we
have ever made it before.

Thus, if it should happen that I fall into sin on the very
day on which I have enjoyed a grace of deep prayer, this does
not prove that the prayer was only self-deception, nor does
it necessarily mean that God's grace which was with me has

now abandoned me. For the very permission of God which allowed me to sin against my neighbor could, in a sense, have been a blessing. For my fall may have revealed to me how weak and imperfect I really am by myself; it may have shown me in a deeply experiential way how shallow my love for God really has been; it may have manifested that I have not yet given myself to God in the totality of my being, from every level of my existence, with my whole heart and soul and mind and strength.

Perhaps in the depths of my spirit where God is found I really did experience the presence of God in my moments of prayer or eucharistic intimacy. But when I returned to more superficial levels of my being, as I went about my daily work and came into conflict with my neighbor, in weakness I fell. Though my situation in regard to my neighbor called for a new gift of myself to God by giving myself to him (and I ought to have been able to do it in the strength of my previous experiences of God), I failed to make the gift of self, I did not give myself on this level of my existence.

By my fall, and in my dawning repentance for it, it was brought home to me once again that God wants the totality of my life and being, not just the "fine point" of my spirit where I meet him in the deeper experiences of explicit prayer. He desires that everything I do and every human relationship in which I engage should be an expression of love for him.

Thus my sin against my neighbor even after I had prayed does not prove that the prayer was merely self-deception and that therefore I should stop praying if I wish to be authentic. My sin certainly shows that I do not yet love God with the totality of my being, with my whole heart and soul and mind and strength, it shows that my gift of self to him is not yet complete. But it does not necessarily mean that he had not truly given himself to me in the grace of prayer, nor does it mean that I had not given myself to him in response, surrendering myself to him in that grace of prayer. It does show, however, that I still have a long way to go in my spiritual combat; it does mean that the Lord will have to continue to pursue me with his invitations of love, his calls to prayer and to repeated conversion.

It is very wrong, then, for me to abandon prayer in discouragement over my sins. My continuing human weaknesses and my sins do not necessarily mean that my prayer has been hypocrisy and self-deception, and that therefore, for the sake of authenticity, I must abandon prayer till I have straightened out all my faults.

On the contrary, even though my repeated failures show that the graces of prayer and of Eucharistic participation do not work as infallible magic in correcting my moral defects but call for my responsible cooperation, still my responsible action in conquering my sins and in loving my neighbor can fully succeed only by the grace of continuing prayer and sacramental participation.

To abandon prayer just because I have sinned or have not yet fulfilled all my social responsibilities, or to claim that because I have failed my prayer must have been hypocrisy and self-deception, is, we said, an insult to the Holy Spirit who gives graces of prayer even to men who are sinners, thus inviting them to an ever fuller conversion.

In times of failure and discouragement, far from doubting or denying the reality of my past experiences of God in prayer, I should gratefully remember these experiences and give thanks to God for them, for they were a pledge of his everlasting love for me though I was still such a weak human being; they were an invitation to continue to seek him even from the midst of my failures; they contained promise of greater graces to come if I would continue to respond to them in times of darkness as well as in times of light. I should remember the love which was concerned about me and was revealing itself to me long before I learned from the sad experience of sin how weak I really am and how much I need that love. I should praise that love which continues to be concerned about me now that I do know my weakness, that love which is ready to lift me up if I continue to seek him in humility, even though of myself I am so unworthy of his love.

This remembrance of my prayerful experiences of God in the past will save me from discouragement over my sins and from a lethal loss of self-esteem. For though I am a sinner, the remembrance of the love which the faithful God has shown me in the past will give me a sense of self-worth, bringing me the courage to start over again in repentance and renewed love.

The experience of my sinful helplessness and the remembrance of God's love for me will give rise in me to anagogical love—the love which humbly reaches to God in faith and hope and finds courage and healing strength in him. Thus discouragement is defeated and the prayer of anagogical love conquers my sinfulness.[49]

Thus, even in my condition as a sinner I must pray, and my prayer will not be self-deception. For in the faith, hope,

---

[49] Anagogical love is described in "Spiritual Sayings Attributed to John of the Cross," *The Complete Works of St. John of the Cross,* III, translated by E. Allison Peers (Westminster, Md.: The Newman Press, 1953), pp. 289–291.

charity and humility which are the ingredients of anagogical love, I truly experience the God of love giving me the grace of prayerful repentance and courageous hope.

Nor will this seeking of intimacy with God even from the depths of my weakness and failings be hypocrisy, for by his grace I will be laboring to master my failings and to be reconciled with the neighbor whom perhaps I have injured by my sin. I must pray for the grace of reconciliation with my brother. I must prayerfully mediate upon ways of resolving my conflict with him. I must think out what is wrong in my relationships with him. In the presence of the Lord, I must try to discover what is wrong in me as well as what is wrong in my brother. And by meditating upon the Lord's will that I be reconciled with him, I must find the courage to seek the reconciliation.

It is indeed true, then, that I must strive to resolve my conflicts with my fellowmen and I must fulfill my various social responsibilities to the best of my ability if I am to hope for deepening relationships with God. But this does not mean that I must stop praying and receiving the Eucharist until all my relationships with my fellowmen have been completely perfected. The Eucharist will give me grace to bring these relationships to perfection.

Imperfect relationships with my fellowmen do indeed mean imperfect relationships with God—to the extent that these bad relationships with my fellowmen involve guilt on my part. But I will never achieve perfect relationships with God unless even now, while my relationships with him are still poor, I approach him in prayer in the hope of achieving an ever fuller reconciliation with him and my fellowmen.

So pray I must, even when I am a sinner, and my prayer

need not be hypocrisy or self-deception! The prayer of anagogical love is shot through with humility and sincerity. It is weak man's cry of hope to the God of love and reconciliation.

This prayer of hope and the grace it wins entails a responsibility—the obligation to mortify the pride, the laziness, the envy, the lust, or whatever it is which stands between me and God or neighbor.

There can be no growth in deeper relationships with God without this effort at mortification of all within me which tends to resist God. But this is not to say that the merciful Lord will not give me authentic graces of prayer even before the total purification of self has been completed. For the very grace of repentance and the effort at continuing conversion is a response to the initiatives of God's love, it is a prayer in response to a taste of his goodness.

To claim, then, that the prayer of a sinner is hypocrisy, and to say that authentic prayer and human sinfulness are incompatible, is to say that prayer is impossible to man on earth. For who among us can say that he is without sin?

In the story of the two men who went up to the temple to pray, it was the prayer of the sinner which Jesus praised as accepted by God. "O God, be merciful to me a sinner!" (Lk. 18:13).

25

FROM IMPLICIT
TO EXPLICIT PRAYER

We have seen how a pagan, through fidelity to conscience, can encounter God and truly have communion with him in grace. We took pains to explain this in order to bring out more clearly how, for every man, fidelity to conscience is always some sort of meeting with God and is therefore at least an implicit prayer.

Thus, those who do know God and Christ clearly often communicate with him and respond to him through conscience without reflecting on what is happening, and so, in a sense, are praying without knowing it. A businessman, for example, who in the midst of negotiations acts justly, constrained by conscience, achieves the purpose of prayer, namely, communion with God.

The value of this implicit prayer, of course, will be in proportion to how well the man's conscience has been formed and to what extent it has been penetrated with faith and enflamed with charity and is led by the Holy Spirit. For our life can be a very shallow prayer or a very profound prayer, depending upon how well it has been orientated to God through faith and love and through prudence, love's insight. Or, one's life can be no prayer at all, or even a sin, if one's conscience is darkened by self-deceptive rationalization.

At any rate, the dictates of conscience are always signs from God, who ceaselessly awaits us in our heart, expecting new responses to himself, new deepenings of our original commitment. Every acceptance of a dictate of conscience is either a hidden, implicit encounter with God, or an explicit meeting with him in which we are conscious of him precisely as God. The right workings of conscience are either an implicit or an explicit prayer.

By its very nature, however, implicit prayer cries out for completion in explicit prayer. For though prayer and conscience are engaged in the one same task—making our whole life a living communion with God in righteous personal relationships—nevertheless their functions remain distinct. The implicit prayer which is a life according to right conscience is not enough. Explicit prayer always remains necessary. One cannot claim, "My life itself is a prayer, and therefore it is not necessary for me to take time for explicit prayer."

We have noted in preceding chapters that when conscience is more and more enlightened by the Word and Spirit of God, its very workings are often an explicit prayer, for the man consciously consults God in his deliberations of conscience. In fact, a conscience can be fully enlightened and mature—and so a life can be truly profound implicit prayer

—only with the help of frequent explicit prayer and consultation of the Word and Spirit.

Moreover, as we are trying to show, implicit prayer calls for its completion in explicit prayer. Prayer, implicit or explicit, is communion with God. But communion consists in personal relationships, and personal relationships in their fullness are not content to remain merely implicit. They strive for the fullness of presence, the fullness of consciousness and love.

Though every following of a dictate of conscience is at least an implicit encounter with God, both the grace and reason impel man to make these encounters ever more explicit. The implicit encounters are intended by God to lead to ever more explicit ones, culminating eventually in the full face-to-face vision of God in glory. The hidden encounters with God in a life according to conscience open a man's heart to explicit ones in explicit prayer. For the "pure heart"—the clear conscience—"sees God" (Mt. 5:8). It presents no impediments when God offers the graces of deeper prayer.

Since each meeting with God in conscience is intended by God to lead to open encounters with him in fuller truth, conscience itself impels man to seek an ever clearer knowledge of the truth. Concerning all men, Vatican II declares: "All men are bound to seek the truth. . . . It is upon the human conscience that these obligations fall and exert their binding force" (*DH* 1). And concerning Christians, it says: "The disciple is bound by a grave obligation toward Christ, his Master, ever more fully to understand the truth received from him" (*DH* 14).

For the interior grace and word of faith, which is too big for human concepts and words, must nevertheless be understood with the help of human concepts if we are to act upon it and live it. Christ himself is the supreme sign from God, the complete expression of the incomprehensible God, and therefore only in Christ can we find the full explicit meaning of the interior encounters with God in grace and conscience. Christ must become ever more fully the light of our conscience, the word of God forming our conscience ever more explicitly and accurately.

Thus the encounters with God in conscience will constantly become more explicit and more fully a prayer and communion with a God who is truly known.

Implicit Encounters in the Scriptures

We have a number of examples in the Scriptures of what is at first a hidden encounter developing into explicit communion with God. In Genesis Eighteen, Abraham receives three traveling strangers with generous hospitality. One of the three somehow seems to be more important than the other two. At first, Abraham addresses this one only as "lord" (in the sense of "sir"), not as "LORD." For they appear to be only human travelers whom he receives with human love, as any right conscience would dictate should be done. But gradually Abraham becomes aware of whom he is entertaining, and before the chapter is ended he is addressing the chief visitor as "LORD," the name of Yahweh, and is engaged in explicit prayer with him (Gen. 18:27, 32–34).

Referring to this incident, and to another in which Lot, too, receives strangers (Gen. 19), Hebrews says: "Let brotherly love continue. Do not neglect to show hospitality to strangers, for thereby some have entertained angels unawares" (Heb. 13:1–2).

Every neighbor of ours, every fellowman, is truly an "angel," a sign sent from God in which he himself is hidden. Every dictate of conscience, indicating our right relationship with our fellowmen and with the rest of the world about us, is such a sign or angel from God in which God himself comes to us. He is either rejected or received; and if he is received with a right and good heart, with a generous response to conscience, then he reveals himself more clearly; that is, he gives himself in grace, he dwells in the man, with the intention of revealing himself ever more clearly to him as he continues to respond to conscience. Thus, through consistent response to conscience, man comes into fuller communion with God.

Another example of an implicit encounter with God developing into a clear and explicit one is the story of the disciples of Emmaus. At the end, when in the breaking of the bread the disciples fully recognize Jesus as Lord, upon reflection they begin to realize that all the while he walked with them, somehow they knew him: "Did not our hearts burn within us while he talked to us on the road, while he opened to us the scriptures?" (Lk. 24:32). God was speaking to them, the same God who waits in every heart, who jealously watches over every man's spirit, who by his Spirit incessantly appeals to every man.

St. Gregory the Great points out beautifully that it was because of their hospitality to a stranger that these men came to know God clearly: "They had to be tested to see whether they could love as a stranger him whom they did not yet love as their God. . . . They were enlightened not by hearing the precepts of God but in doing them."[50]

Thus again, we see how God encounters us in our con-

[50] Homily for Matins, Easter Monday.

science. The sign of his presence in which he speaks to our heart is a call to Christian love. "This ought to be done," says conscience, and in doing it we are opened to receive God.

The Interior Word of Grace

But when God speaks to us in the ought of conscience and awaits our response, he speaks to us at the same time in an actual grace. We cannot make a response to God except through a gift of interior grace. Thus, God was working by grace in the hearts of the disciples of Emmaus—their hearts were burning within them—even before it occurred to them to urge their hospitality upon the stranger. God always takes the initiative if there is to be either an implicit or explicit encounter with him. And the human situation of conscience clarifies for us what the interior grace is saying.

Therefore, only by a prevenient grace of God can a man, following the urgings of conscience, make the option in which, implicitly, he chooses God as the goal of his life and hence is given the grace of justification, or an increase of sanctifying grace. For even the beginnings of justification are a grace from God. Only an actual grace, some sort of interior light or urging from God, can bring conscience to pronounce that impelling *ought* which, when obeyed with the help of grace, brings in the very act of obedience the grace of justification, or an increase of grace in a man already just.

"I will manifest myself to him" (Jn. 14:21)

Their hearts were burning within them, though they did not yet explicitly recognize God in their companion. We can be praying and not even know it; we can be in true communion with God without realizing it; God can be speaking his interior word in our heart before we are fully aware of what is happening.

However, every such hidden encounter with God, we said, is intended by him to lead us to an increasingly explicit communion with him. The meeting with God through love of neighbor, or through some other choice in conscience, or through some interior urging of grace, is intended to lead one on to pure prayer, to explicit communion with God. God is not content to meet us only in a hidden way in our neighbor. Personal relationships in love are not content to remain implicit.

Abraham's hidden encounters with God in a stranger led to an encounter with him in explicit prayer, and the disciples of Emmaus, receiving a stranger, came to a direct meeting with Jesus, the Lord God himself. Jesus promises a similar direct meeting with the three Persons of the Holy Trinity to anyone who keeps his word (Jn. 14:15–23).

The whole context in which this promise is made—the Last Supper discourse—shows that by "his word," "his commandments," what is especially meant is the "new commandment": "Love one another as I have loved you" (Jn. 13:34; 15:12).

The *Holy Spirit,* whom the world cannot receive or know, will be known by those who keep this commandment, for he will dwell in them (Jn. 14:15–17). And *Jesus* will manifest himself in a new way to those who keep this commandment, for he will dwell in them (Jn. 14:18–21). And when Judas (not Iscariot) asks Jesus how he will manifest himself to them, Jesus tells him that it will be an interior manifestation of Themselves by the indwelling three divine Persons: "If a man loves me, he will keep my word, and my *Father* will love him, and *we* will come to him and make our home with him" (Jn. 14:22–23).

A direct meeting with the indwelling Trinity is thus promised to the man who first meets God in neighbor through effective fraternal love.

We cannot explain the promised manifestation of the three divine Persons only on the level of active love of neighbor; the encounter with the Trinity cannot be limited to the implicit encounter with God as manifest in our neighbor, the sign of God. For the love of our neighbor is here presented by Jesus as a *predisposition* to an interior encounter, a contemplative experience of the indwelling Three. When the Christian keeps the word of Jesus, the command to love our neighbor, he is open to the Holy Spirit who comes to him in a new interior mission, taking fuller possession of him than before and dwelling more completely in him; and the Christian *knows* him; and the Word, in a new interior mission, *manifests* himself to him; and the Father also comes and *dwells* in him, and is embraced in filial love in the Holy Spirit.

Thus, those who love God as present to them in their neighbors are invited by Jesus to expect, and also to seek, a direct contemplative experience of the Holy Trinity. To this interior revelation and self-communication of God the Christian is expected to pay explicit attention.

To maintain that we meet God only in our neighbor, and that a direct encounter with him in prayer and contemplation is unnecessary, is an unjustifiable impoverishment of the Christian experience; it is to ignore the witness of countless Christian men and women throughout the ages who have testified to the contemplative experience.

We must not be content, then, to encounter God only

implicitly, as present to us only in our neighbor; he wishes to encounter us explicitly in his personal dwelling within us. The implicit encounter with him in our neighbor invites us to explicit prayer and purifies our hearts for it.

"Called as a Son to commune with God" (GS 21)

Vatican II implies all of this in a statement in its section on atheism in *Gaudium et Spes*. The atheistic humanism of our times has reinterpreted Christian truths in an atheistic way. Atheism no longer attacks Christianity directly by attempting to refute it by methods of logic. It has a more deceptive strategy. It does not deny that there is truth in the Christian mysteries, but claims to understand and explain this truth more profoundly. It does not deny the attributes of God, but transfers them to man, their true owner. Christ is only a symbol of every man's struggle for fulfillment, for growth toward the ideal, symbolized as a god.[51]

These atheists claim that the way Christians used to understand their mysteries was a necessary stage in the development of human consciousness. But now that man has come of age, now that he can do for himself what he used to expect from God, he can attribute to himself the perfections he used to attribute to God. To encounter our fellowman is to encounter God. Indeed, human society *is* God.

Hence, instead of the Christian way of finding God present to men in the sign, the community of men united in love, the community is substituted for God. This deception has entrapped only too many Christians who, while still holding

[51] Henri de Lubac, "Nature and Grace," in Burke, *The Word in History*, pp. 28–29.

to the existence of a personal God who transcends human society, maintain that because they find God in their fellow-men there is no need for explicit prayer.

The atheistic humanist rejects God as a transcendent Person because such a God seems to be a threat to human intelligence and freedom, a threat to the human person.

Vatican II reacts to these various claims of atheistic humanism (and therefore to the deception into which some Christians have fallen) when it declares: "Man was made an intelligent and free member of society by the God who created him, but even more important, he is called as a son to commune with God and share in his happiness" (*GS* 21). The social nature of man, calling for respect for each human person, for the recognition of every man as a brother, calls also for the recognition of God as Father. God is not human society. He is a personal God infinitely transcending society, which is a sign in which he wishes to manifest his presence through the love of men for one another.

But the human social dimension—the so-called horizontal dimension—is not enough. Man is not merely a brother among brothers; "he is called as a son to commune with God." He is to have a direct relationship in Christ with the Father in heaven. "Christ has risen, destroying death by his death. He has lavished life upon us, so that as sons in the Son, we can cry out in the Spirit, 'Abba, Father!' " (*GS* 22).

In other words, the dictate of conscience requiring us to recognize and treat every man as our brother is an implicit invitation from God to recognize him as Father. When a man accepts this invitation by accepting his brother in effective love, then God accepts him as a son by pouring into him his Holy Spirit: "If anyone love me, he will keep my word . . . and we will come to him and make our abode with him" (Jn. 14:23). Man is thus empowered to come into direct, explicit encounter with the Father. Because we have responded to God's invitation to find him hidden in our neighbor, the sign of God, we have received the Holy Spirit in whom we can have direct contact with God in faith, hope and love in a prayerful experience of his indwelling Presence. We must, of course, consciously cultivate the awareness of this God who dwells in us and wishes to manifest himself in the graces of prayer.

For the grace of the divine indwelling is a subtle interior grace which will be lost upon us if we do not cultivate an attentiveness to it. In this prayer of attentiveness to the indwelling God, with the help of grace, I bring to the level of explicit consciousness the various relationships to the three divine Persons in which I have been established by the gift of sanctifying grace. I become in consciousness what I am in ontic reality—a dwelling of the Holy Spirit, a member of Christ, an adoptive son of the Father, and a brother of all my brothers in Christ.

What I thus acknowledge in the interiority of my prayer-life I express in the totality of my daily life, and especially in my relationships with my fellowmen in fraternal love. After my explicit meetings with the Father in prayer, my subsequent implicit meetings with him in my neighbor are all the more valuable, my life as a prayer has all the more worth—for my conscience is now perfected with a deeper faith and charity.

26

BE SPIRITED IN THE SPIRIT

Only a man of the Spirit can possess the wisdom of God: the insight and decision necessary for living according to "the mind of the Lord" (1 Cor. 2:16), the intention of his salvific will.

Therefore, the basic Christian endeavor is to come ever more fully under the influence of the Holy Spirit. St. Paul frequently summons us to this. "If we live by the Spirit, then let us walk by the Spirit" (Gal. 5:25). If the Spirit is the source of our life, let us conduct ourselves accordingly.

This summons to action in the Spirit is a call to action which is simultaneously his action and ours. The apostle's exhortation amounts to this: The Holy Spirit is the whole source of your moral and spiritual life. From him alone comes your power to discern the mind of God and to act accordingly. And yet, when you walk by the Spirit, when you

live by his power, it is your action even while it is his. As
you grow in the Spirit, more and more you absorb the Holy
Spirit into your spirit, and your action becomes ever more
divine.

Thus St. Paul exhorts the Romans to renewal in the Spirit:
"Do not be conformed to this world, but be transformed by
the renewal of your mind, that you may prove what is the
will of God, what is good and acceptable and perfect" (Rom.
12:2). When you respond to this exhortation, it is you who
discern God's mind, his purpose; and the decisions you make
in this light are your personal decisions; and the action
according to these decisions is your action. And yet, all of
this is also and primarily the work of the Holy Spirit who is
in you as your life. He is the light of your Christian conscience.

The Holy Spirit becomes, as it were, "built into" our
mind, into our consciousness, into the very structure of our
personality. We become so used to turning to him for light
that his light more and more becomes our permanent personal light.

Therefore when St. Paul says, "Be renewed in the spirit
of your mind" (Eph. 4:23), by "mind" he means "the interior man" (Eph. 3:16), the religious and moral personality
as regenerated by the Holy Spirit—the intelligence, the will,
the affections, the conscience, the faculties of moral perception and discernment.[52] He means all these moral and religious powers as integrated and unified in their functioning
by the Holy Spirit, orientated in the right direction and toward the right action, and impelled into this action by an
inner spirit or life.

[52] Ceslaus Spicq, *Théologie Morale du Nouveau Testament*, p. 680,
note 3.

St. Paul prays for us that the Holy Spirit will do this for us, and he appeals to us to bring it about. It is the Spirit's work and it is our work. He prays: "I bow my knees before the Father . . . that he may grant you to be strengthened with might through his Spirit in the inner man" (Eph. 3:16). And he tells *us* to bring this about: "Be renewed in the spirit of your mind" (Eph. 4:23). Only the Holy Spirit can do it, but he can do it only if we do it with him. For this renewal, this orientation of the spirit of our mind, is the turning of our own free will. It is we who turn, the decision is ours. And yet it is the work of the Holy Spirit.

If we do not go to work in the Holy Spirit, there will be no spiritual action of ours, no spiritual renewal. We will not become morally and spiritually mature, true masters of our actions.

The work of spiritual renewal, then, the structuring of our spirituality, our moral and religious personality, is our work as well as the Spirit's work, and without our work it will not be accomplished.

Paul's exhortation, then, "Be renewed in the spirit of your mind," amounts to saying, "Be spirited in the Holy Spirit!" For in biblical language, whereas the word "soul" simply means life, the word "spirit" means power and intensity of life. The Spirit of God in the Christian is the source of his properly Christian vitality.[53]

"Be renewed in the spirit of your mind" means "Come alive in the Holy Spirit—be spirited in the Spirit of God!"

But this renewal is not accomplished in an instant. In the Greek, grammatically, St. Paul's expression "be renewed" is a present tense of continuity.[54] The integrating and matur-

[53] *Ibid.,* p. 85, note 3.
[54] *Ibid.,* p. 680, note 5.

ing of our personality in the Holy Spirit is a continuing process, to be worked at persistently. It begins in baptism, but is continued and perfected by our personal efforts in cooperation with the Holy Spirit.

To the extent that this work of renewal in the Spirit is accomplished in us, we have "the mind of Christ." God's own wisdom or purpose is built into our personality and spirituality in a dynamic way. By this renewal, our personality is so structured, so integrated, so orientated that we grow ever more fully toward the freedom, the complete self-possession, of the children of God. Our personality is ever supple, open, alert, alive with a divine light and power. It is spirited in the Holy Spirit, the Spirit of the Son who makes us sons of God in *the* Son.

In our full freedom as sons of God, we are fully turned toward the Father in love's free choice, for the love of God has been poured into our hearts by the Holy Spirit who has been given to us. Living in our hearts—that is, in our interior self, at the very root of the complex of faculties which are the seat of our moral action—the Spirit orientates the vital force of our spirit to the Father in the great cry of love, "Abba!"

Thus we have love's liberty—everything we do is inspired by love of the Father and of our brothers and sisters in Christ. "Where the Spirit of the Lord is, there is freedom" (2 Cor. 3:17). The orientation of our inner man, our whole personality, to the Father in the love formed in us by the Holy Spirit liberates us from the narrow egoistic darkness of the unspiritual man to whom the wisdom of God is folly. And this love, integrating and unifying our interior powers in a thrust toward God, liberates us from the slavery of un-

controlled passions, saves us from dissipating our vital power
in all directions, ending in frustration.

All our moral effort, then, should be directed toward
coming ever more fully under the influence of the Holy
Spirit: "Be renewed in the spirit of your mind, and put on
the new man" (Eph. 4:23).

In what practical ways can we accomplish this? The clue to
the answer is in a parallel passage, to the Colossians, where
St. Paul expresses the same thought in slightly different
words: "Strip off the old man with his deeds and put on the
new, one that is being renewed unto perfect knowledge
'according to the image of his Creator' " (Col. 3:9-10, c).
Christ is the image of the Creator, we are told in an earlier
passage: "He is the image of the invisible God" (Col. 1:15, c).

Our renewal unto perfect knowledge according to the
image of the Creator—our growth in moral insight—consists
therefore in more and more perfectly acquiring "the mind of
Christ" (1 Cor. 2:16), his attitudes, his intentions; and especially his basic attitude as Son of the Father: humble obedience. "Have this mind in you which was also in Christ
Jesus. . . . He humbled himself, becoming obedient unto
death, even to death on a cross. . . ." (Phil. 2:5-8, c). "I do
always the things that please the Father," he said (Jn. 8:29).

Our efforts, then, in carrying on the incessant process of
renewal of the spirit of our mind should be a persistent
search for God's true will in every situation, a seeking to do
always the things that please him. In repeated interior cries
to the Holy Spirit, we ask his light for discerning God's will.
We thus become so accustomed to turning to the Spirit and
walking in the Spirit that he becomes the permanent light of
our conscience, as it were fully absorbed into our spirit. He
no longer remains hidden in the depths of our soul as only

a root of the divine life we hope for, but is ever active and fruitful in our spirit by his graces. We become fully spirited in the Spirit.

All of this comes about in a paradoxical way—in a seeming contradiction. For, we have seen, it is in self-surrender to the Holy Spirit that we are most mature. In explaining this, St. Paul spoke of a childishness, an immaturity which consisted in being closed to the Holy Spirit, incapable of receiving his true wisdom because of narrow pride and self-sufficiency. Maturity, on the other hand, is complete openness to the Holy Spirit, complete surrender to him in humility.

But this very maturity, this humble openness to the Spirit, is described by Jesus as being childlike. Being childlike in our Lord's sense is the very opposite of that childish immaturity of proud resistance described by St. Paul. Therefore there is perfect agreement between Jesus saying "Become as little children" and Paul saying "Brethren, do not be children in your thinking; be babes in evil, but in thinking be mature" (1 Cor. 14:20).

This maturity in thinking, this spiritual insight, is the divine wisdom of the humble little ones to whom the Father has seen fit to reveal the secrets hidden from the so-called wise and prudent (Lk. 10:21). "I would have you wise as to what is good," says Paul, "and guileless as to what is evil" (Rom. 16:19). "Be wise as serpents," said Jesus, "and innocent as doves" (Mt. 10:16).

Paradoxically, then, the spiritual childhood recommended by Jesus opens us to the highest maturity in the Holy Spirit. They who are surrendered to the Holy Spirit in humility are formed by the Holy Spirit to cry "Father!" in all their actions. They know the wisdom of God, which is the foolishness of the cross. They have brought their minds into captivity to Christ (2 Cor. 10:5) and have found the liberty of the children of God. "Where the Spirit of the Lord is, there is freedom" (2 Cor. 3:17).

In every situation, then, we must consciously search out God's true will, calling for the light of the Holy Spirit; and he will come to reside ever more fully in our consciousness as the full light of our conscience. And we will always be spirited with the Spirit of God.

27

"THEY WILL SOAR
AS WITH EAGLES' WINGS"

"Be renewed in the spirit of your mind"; "Be spirited in the Holy Spirit!" Find in him your full Christian vitality. Let him reside ever more fully in your personality as in his living temple, so that he will be the full light of your conscience.

This renewal in the Spirit brings more than divine light and insight. It brings a wonderful moral strength and stamina, an undaunted courage and firmness in carrying out love's enlightened decisions. St. Paul prayed that we might have this fortitude in the Holy Spirit, saying, "I bend my knees to the Father . . . that he may grant you from his glorious riches to be strengthened with power through his Spirit unto the progress of the inner man" (Eph. 3:14–16, c).

We shall better understand how to acquire this strength in the Holy Spirit—for our spiritual renewal is our work as well as his—if we look into the cause of the opposite weakness, the cause of the dissipation of the energies of our moral and spiritual life.

The Departure from the Divine Presence

St. Paul describes the renewal in the Spirit as our restoration in the image and likeness of God: "Strip off the old man with his deeds and put on the new, one that is being renewed unto perfect knowledge 'according to the image of his Creator'" (Col. 3:9, c). The image of God in man was distorted when man sought knowledge through disobedience, eating of the forbidden tree of knowledge of good and evil, trying to be a law unto himself. Instead of knowledge, he found darkness. He became unspiritual, incapable of perceiving the divine wisdom which only the Holy Spirit can give.

It was not Adams's sin alone which spoiled God's image in mankind; it was also done by the personal sins of generation after generation of Adam's descendants, which ratified and deepened the original sin. In the Bible, man's moral weakness is shown as resulting from his break with God. When by sin man ruptured his communion with God and went out from the divine presence, then relationships between man and man quickly deteriorated. Man turned against his wife— Adam blamed Eve for his troubles; brother rose against brother—Cain envied Abel and killed him. Nation rose against nation—the peoples who before had been of one mind, one speech, were divided and scattered abroad through the pride of Babel.

Nor was there only the disintegration of personal relationships among men; a similar disintegration took place within man himself when he cut himself off from communion with

God. In fact, the disintegration within man gave rise to the social disintegration: "Whence do wars and quarrels come among you? Is it not from this, from your passions which wage war in your members? You covet and do not have; you kill and envy, and cannot obtain" (Jas. 4:1–2, c).

St. Paul sums up in a word the spiritual and moral helplessness of unredeemed, disintegrated man, man without the Spirit of God. Speaking in the person of fallen mankind, he says: "To wish is within my power, but I do not find the strength to accomplish what is good" (Rom. 8:18, c).

And all because man went out from the divine Presence, all because by sin he destroyed his loving communion with God. When man no longer lives in the divine Presence, in vital communion with God, he becomes steadily weaker, his spiritual and moral vitality degenerates, his personality and his personal relationships disintegrate. This is evident from St. Paul's description in Romans 1:18–32 of the degenerate state of the pagan world. The multitude of sins against nature and neighbor which he lists all stem from man's refusal to acknowledge God and give him thanks.

The Return of the Divine Presence

With the call of Abraham, man is invited back into the life-giving divine Presence. The Lord says to Abraham, "Walk in my presence and be perfect" (Gen. 17:1, c). Adam could not bear to be in the divine Presence after his sin, and tried to hide himself. Abraham is instructed to live blamelessly so that he can be at ease in the presence of God and live in loving communion with him. With Abraham's call, mankind's journey back into the divine Presence begins in earnest, for God's love has issued the invitation. The journey is completed only in the Person of Jesus, Son of Abraham, Son of God, when he returns to the Father in his paschal mystery, opening the way for all to follow.

All this salvation history is the background of St. Paul's exhortation: "You are to put off the old man which is being corrupted through its deceptive lusts; but be renewed in the spirit of your mind, and put on the new man . . . one that is being renewed unto perfect knowledge 'according to the image of his Creator' " (Eph. 3:22–24 with Col. 3:9, c).

In other words, put on the likeness of Jesus, Son and Image of the invisible God. Only thus can the image and likeness of God, distorted by sin, be restored. This means putting on "the mind of Christ"—the likeness of our Lord's loving obedience to the Father. But even more profoundly, it means entering into our Lord's communion with the Father, his loving presence with the Father, and thus recovering the moral and spiritual vitality which was lost when man disrupted his communion with God. To be renewed according to Christ, the image of the Creator, is to be renewed in the likeness of his communion with the Father in the Holy Spirit.

"He will renew you in his love"

The prophet Sophonia had spoken of this renewal of man through his re-establishment in the divine Presence:

> Fear not, O Sion, be not discouraged!
> > The Lord your God is in your midst,
> > A mighty Saviour.
> He will rejoice over you with gladness,
> > And renew you in his love (Soph. 3:17, c).

"Abide in my love," said Jesus (Jn. 15:10). "Abide in me and I in you . . . for without me you can do nothing" (15:4, 6, c).

Moral helplessness and disintegration, resulting from loss of communion with God, is turned into spiritual strength when we re-establish our communion with God by abiding in Christ.

"Young men, you are strong"

In his first epistle, St. John speaks specifically of the spiritual strengthening which results from abiding in Christ by keeping his word. "Young men," he writes, "I addressed you because you are strong, and the word of God abides in you, and you have conquered the Evil One" (1 Jn. 2:14, c).

You are strong because the word of God abides in you and in this strength you have conquered the Evil One. John is not speaking of the strength of physical youth but of the spiritual vigor which comes from communion with God in the keeping of his word.

This passage refers back not only to our Lord's discourse at the Last Supper—abide in me—but also to the good news of Isaia concerning spiritual renewal. Isaia tells how even young men in their full physical vigor grow faint and weary in discouragement when they are deprived of moral and spiritual strength; but God promises their renewal:

> Do you not know
>   Or have you not heard?
> The Lord is the eternal God,
>   creator of the ends of the earth.

> He does not faint nor grow weary,
>   and his knowledge is beyond scrutiny.
> He gives strength to the fainting;
>   for the weak he makes vigor abound.
> Though young men faint and grow weary,
>   and youths stagger and fall,
> They that hope in the Lord will renew their strength,
>   they will soar as with eagles' wings;
> They will run and not grow weary,
>   walk and not grow faint (Isa. 40:28–31, c).

Earlier in the same chapter Isaia had shown the source of this renewal of strength: the word of the Lord which endures forever.

> All mankind is grass
>   And all their glory is like the flower of the field.
> The grass withers, the flower wilts,
>   When the breath of the Lord blows upon it. . . .
> Though the grass withers and the flower wilts,
>   the word of our God stands forever (Isa. 40:6–8, c).

Writing to the young men who are strong because the word of God abides in them, St. John says, "The man who does God's will endures forever" (1 Jn. 2:17, nc). The word of our God endures forever—the man who does God's will endures forever. For he embraces and keeps the word which expresses God's will; and Jesus, the Word, dwells in him. "If anyone love me, he will keep my word . . . and we will come to him" (Jn. 14:23).

St. John goes on to describe the victory won by the young men who are strong because the word of God abides in them. It is a victory over the Evil One who attacks men through their own inner weakness, i.e., through the triple concupiscence in them which draws them to the world and away from love of the Father:

Have no love for the world, nor for the things the world affords. For not a thing that the world affords comes from the Father: carnal allurements, eye-catching enticements, the glamorous life—all this comes from the world itself. And the world is passing away with all its charms, but the man who does God's will endures forever (1 Jn. 2:15–17, nc).

The three concupiscences described by John—the concupiscence of the flesh, the concupiscence of the eyes, and the pride of life; or, in the translation we have just quoted, "carnal allurements, eye-catching enticements, the glamorous life"—are but three different concrete expressions of one concupiscence. For concupiscence is nothing else than egotism.

Concupiscence manifests itself in the pursuit of good things in an evil manner. It consists in the tendency to make of earthly goods something absolute, a god, whether these be the goods of the body, or external riches, or fame and honor. It is the tendency to serve mammon rather than God. Or even more profoundly, concupiscence is the love of self carried even to the contempt of God. It prefers self to God, and fashions one in the image and likeness of Satan, who said, "I will not serve!"

By preferring self to God, destroying communion with God, concupiscence results in an enslaving weakness. Man helplessly falls victim to the enticing allurements of the flesh, or of riches, or of ambition and vain display. Man becomes torn by conflicting desires, and unable to do the good he wishes to do.

The remedy for this weakness is embracing God's word, accepting his will: "Young men, you are strong because the word of God abides in you. The man who does God's will endures forever." Or, to return to St. Paul's expression of the same truth: "Be renewed according to the image of your Creator"—be renewed in Christ's obedience to the word and will of the Father.

The Soaring Eagle

St. John himself has become a symbol of the perpetual youth which is found by abiding in Christ—as in the extra-biblical story which tells of his being thrown into boiling oil for bearing witness to the Word of Christ and coming out more youthful than ever. "Though young men faint and grow weary, and youths stagger and fall, they that hope in the Lord will renew their strength, they will soar as with eagles' wings."

The eagle has become the symbol of St. John, who soared in faith to the eternal heights and found the Word in the presence of the Father: "In the beginning was the Word, and the Word was in God's presence, and the Word was God" (Jn. 1:1, nc). And the Word became flesh and dwelt among us, and returned to the Father, bringing us into that presence. St. John, abiding in the Word, took on the eternal vigor of the Son of God.

Thoughts like these must have inspired the cry attributed to St. Augustine: "O young man, seek Christ, that you may remain perpetually young!"[55]

The older we get—that is, the more spiritually mature

[55] "Quaerite ergo, O juvenes, Christum, ut juvenes maneatis" (PL 40:1319).

through an ever more perfect surrender to the Holy Spirit—
the more youthful we become in the eternal youth of Christ,
the immortal Word who endures forever. As we abide in him
by letting his word abide in us, pondering it in our hearts
and expressing it in our lives, as we nourish ourselves by
abiding in his Eucharistic Presence, he renews us in his likeness by an ever more abundant share in his Holy Spirit, who
impels us into the presence of God, crying, "Abba, Father!"

> Fear not, O Sion, be not discouraged!
> The Lord your God is in your midst,
> a mighty Saviour.
> He will rejoice over you with gladness,
> And renew you in his love.

*Imprimi Potest: Gilbert J. Graham, O.P., March 25, 1969; Nihil Obstat:
Leo J. Steady, Ph.D., S.T.D., Censor Librorum; Imprimatur; †Robert
F. Joyce, Bishop of Burlington, May 14, 1969. The Nihil Obstat and
Imprimatur are a declaration that a book or pamphlet is considered to
be free from doctrinal or moral error. It is not implied that those who
have granted the Nihil Obstat and Imprimatur agree with the contents, opinions or statements expressed.*